COUNTRY CRAFTS
& COOKING

COUNTRY CRAFTS & COOKING

Inspirational ideas for natural gifts, decorations ❧ and recipes ❧

TESSA EVELEGH, KATHERINE RICHMOND, AND LIZ TRIGG

PHOTOGRAPHS BY

MICHELLE GARRETT

HH
HERMES HOUSE

This edition first published in 1997 by Hermes House
27 West 20th Street, New York, NY 10011

HERMES HOUSE books are available for bulk purchase for sales promotion and for
premium use. For details, write or call the sales director,
Hermes House, 27 West 20th Street, New York, NY 10011;
(800) 354-9657

Hermes House is an imprint of Anness Publishing Limited

ISBN 1-901289-50-8

Publisher: Joanna Lorenz
Project Editor: Christopher Fagg
Editor: Lydia Darbyshire
Designer: Siân Keogh
Photographers: Michelle Garrett, Lucy Mason, Gloria Nicol

Printed and bound in Singapore

This book was previously published as part of a larger compendium, *Country*.

Contributors: Fiona Barnett, Tessa Evelegh, Caroline Kelly, Katherine Richmond, Zoe Smith,
Isabel Stanley, Liz Trigg, Jenny Watson, Dorothy Wood

1 3 5 7 9 10 8 6 4 2

Contents

Introduction

 Everyone dreams of an idealized world where the pressures of modern life slip away, days are full of sunshine, vegetables are harvested fresh from the garden, fruit hangs from bushes and trees, an old fruit press squeezes out fresh apple juice in the barn and the house is full of flowers, the scent of thyme and lavender and the heady smell of freshly baking bread. It may not be possible to realize this dream; not everyone wants to live that close to nature, but many people would like to bring a small part of country peace and tranquility into the pressurized existence of the late twentieth century.

One way this can be achieved is through the recreation of country crafts and using country recipes in the kitchen. This has a twofold benefit. The practice of country crafts produces an atmosphere of calm and truth within the household. Making lavender bags, for instance, which scent clothes and deter moths so beautifully, is both practical and useful, but it also means that less attention is paid to the gods of twentieth-century living – the television and radio – and in a small way, it increases the spirituality of life.

Country Crafts and Cooking sets out a number of the traditional country craft projects that can be practiced in every home, be it in the depths of the country or in the heart of the city. Concentrating on traditional herbal recipes and remedies taken from old country folklore, the first part of the book outlines many ideas that are both practical and therapeutic. Among the easiest are the old-fashioned pomanders, so useful for scenting rooms and clothes, and there are also cleansing lotions, hair tonic and aftershave, herbal pots and sleep pillows and many other country-style gifts suitable for Christmas, Easter and Thanksgiving. These country tokens all have a practical use and can be created by anyone who wishes to bring a touch of country to their home.

All the projects call for traditional country ingredients that can nowadays be gathered in the garden or readily bought in local markets. They are all simple and satisfying.

Country cooking goes hand in hand with country crafts. Country cooking is a state of mind, a determination not to succumb to the prepackaged, prefabricated ready meals so easily available in supermarkets and stores but to produce food that really tastes like food, that tastes like the country and that uses fresh ingredients in season at the right time of the year.

This is simpler if you have a vegetable garden where you can grow your own fruit and vegetables, but it can be practiced by any cook who is determined enough to search out the best and freshest ingredients in markets and to use only those when preparing food for the family.

The mouthwatering recipes in this book are divided into the four seasons of the year, which determine the rhythm of country living. In the spring come the first fresh young vegetables, spring chicken and lamb and dishes embellished with fresh leeks and onions. The summer brings mint and herbs, used to make fresh mint ice cream, the first strawberries of the year, delicious new potatoes dug straight from the earth and tender young beans and asparagus, while autumn is also a time of plenty. There are apples on the trees and blackberries in the hedges, mushrooms in the fields and a cornucopia of vegetables to be harvested. In the winter as the nights draw in and the family gathers around the fire, the country cook concentrates on traditional stews, thick, warming lentil soups, and the festive Christmas puddings and shortbread.

The country year is seen more clearly in the kitchen than anywhere else in the house, and the recipes in *Country Crafts and Cooking* will provide a rich source of inspiration to help you create a warm, welcoming atmosphere. So follow your instincts and enjoy the charm of country life.

COUNTRY
Crafts

Tokens to Treasure

....

What can bring more pleasure than gifts inspired by country traditions? They have a quality that acknowledges the seasons and withstands the test of time. Gather together all the natural materials you can find — shells, papers, natural fabrics, wire, and even chickenwire — and turn them into something very special.

Sleep Pillow

Many people still swear by sleep pillows, which are traditionally filled with chamomile and hops. Since hops are related to the cannabis plant, they induce a feeling of sleepy well-being, while chamomile helps you to relax. Either buy ready-prepared sleep mix, or make up your own with chamomile, lemon verbena and a few hops. Stitch a pillow filled with these relaxing herbs to keep on your bed, and look forward to a good night's sleep.

MATERIALS

*linen muslin, 80 × 8 in
(this can be made up of two
or more shorter lengths)
pins, needle and thread
scissors
pure cotton fabric, 20 × 10 in
herbal sleep mix
39 in antique lace
39 in ribbon, ½ in wide
4 pearl buttons*

1

Prepare the linen muslin border by stitching together enough lengths to make up 80 in. With right sides facing, stitch the ends together to form a ring. Trim the seam. Fold the ring in half lengthwise with wrong sides facing and run a line of gathering stitches close to the raw edges.

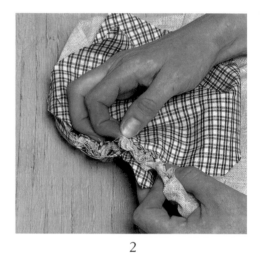

2

Cut two pieces of cotton fabric into 10 in squares. Pull up the gathering threads of the muslin to fit the cushion edge. Pin it to the right side of one square, with raw edges facing outwards, matching the raw edges and easing the gathers evenly round the cushion. Put the second square on top and pin the corners. Stitch the seams, leaving a gap for stuffing. Trim the seams.

3

Turn the cushion rightside out and fill it with herbal sleep mix. Stitch the gap to enclose the border.

4

Using tiny stitches, sew the lace to the cushion about 1 in away from the border.

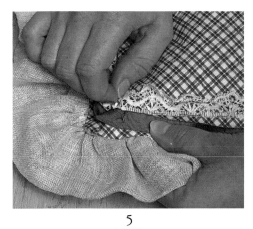

5

Stitch the ribbon close to the lace, making a neat diagonal fold at the corners.

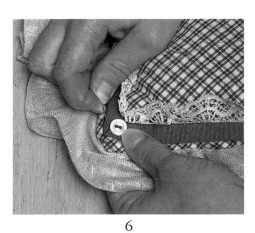

6

Finish by sewing a tiny pearl button to each corner.

Herb Pot-holder

Protect tabletops from hot pots and pans with an aromatic mat, filled with cinnamon, cloves and bay leaves. The heat of the pot immediately releases the fragrance of its contents, kept evenly distributed with mattress-style ties.

MATERIALS

scissors
mattress ticking, at least
25 × 22 in
pins, needle and thread

spice mix to fill, e.g. dried bay
leaves, cloves, cinnamon sticks
heavyduty upholstery needle
cotton string

1

First make the hanger by cutting a strip of ticking 2 × 12 in. With right sides facing, fold this in half lengthwise. Stitch the long side, leaving the ends open. Trim the seam. Turn right side out and press. Fold in half to form a loop. Cut two rectangles from the fabric measuring about 25 × 20 in.

2

Place the cushion pieces on a flat surface, right sides facing, and then slip the hanging loop between the layers, with the raw edges pointing out towards a corner.

3

Pin and stitch the cushion pieces together, leaving about 3 in open. Trim the seams. Turn right side out.

4

Fill the cushion with the spices.

5

Slip-stitch to close the opening.

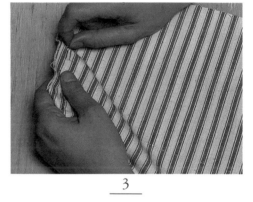

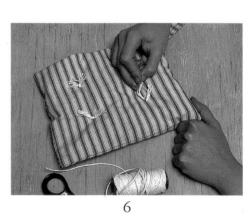

6

Using a heavyduty upholstery needle threaded with cotton string, make a stitch about a third in from two sides of the cushion, clearing the spices inside the mat away from the area as you go. Untwist the strands of the string for a more feathery look. Repeat with three other ties to give a mattress effect. Make a simple knot in each to secure the ties.

Lavender Sachets

Use fabric scraps to appliqué simple motifs on to charming checked fabrics, and then stitch them into sachets to fill with lavender and use as drawer-fresheners. Inspired by traditional folk art, these have universal appeal.

MATERIALS
scissors
fabric scraps
paper for templates
pins, needle and thread
stranded embroidery thread in different colors
loose dried lavender
button

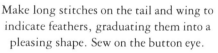

1

Cut two pieces of fabric into squares about 6 in. If you are using a checked or striped fabric, it is a good idea to let the design dictate the exact size. Scale up the template and use it as a pattern to cut bird and wing shapes from contrasting fabrics. Pin and baste the bird shape to the right side of one square.

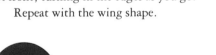

2

Neatly slip-stitch the bird shape to the sachet front, turning in the edges as you go. Repeat with the wing shape.

3

Using three strands of embroidery thread in a contrasting color, make neat running stitches around the bird and its wing.

4

Make long stitches on the tail and wing to indicate feathers, graduating them into a pleasing shape. Sew on the button eye.

5

With right sides facing, stitch the front and back of the sachet together, leaving a 2 in gap. Trim the seams. Turn it right side out and press. Fill with dried lavender, and then slip-stitch to close the gap.

TOKENS TO TREASURE

Lacy Lavender Heart

*Evocative of the Victorian era, this exquisitely pretty heart-shaped lavender bag
is made from simple, creamy muslin, and trimmed with antique lace and
satin ribbon. The chiffon ribbon at the top is tied into a loop for hanging on
coat hangers with favorite garments.*

MATERIALS

paper for template
scissors
silky muslin, about
24 × 8 in

pins, needle and stranded
embroidery thread
pearl button
loose dried lavender

20 in antique lace
20 in very narrow
satin ribbon
20 in medium ribbon

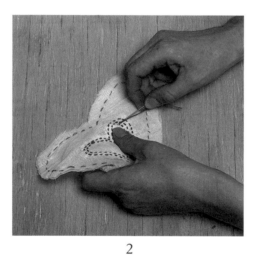

1

Make a heart-shaped paper template about
6 in high and use this as a pattern. Cut
four heart shapes from muslin. Tack the
hearts together in pairs so each heart is a
double thickness of muslin.

2

Cut a smaller heart shape from muslin.
Carefully stitch this to the center front of one
of the larger heart shapes, using two strands
of embroidery thread and a running stitch.
Make another row of running stitches
inside this.

3

Sew the button to the top
of the smaller heart.

4

Stitch a third row of running stitches inside
the other two. Allow the edges of the smaller
heart to fray. With right sides facing, stitch
all around the edge of the two large double-
thickness muslin heart shapes, leaving a gap
of 2 in. Trim the seams, snip into the seam
at the 'V' of the heart and snip off the
bottom point within the seam allowance.
Turn the heart right-side out. Fill it with
lavender and slip-stitch to close the gap.
Don't despair if the heart looks pretty
miserable and misshapen at this stage!

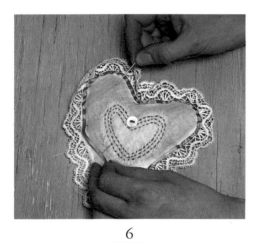

Carefully slip-stitch the lace around the edge
of the heart.

6

Stitch the satin ribbon over the lower edge
of the lace.

7

Finish with a ribbon bow, arranging it so the
long tails are upwards as these can then be
joined to form a loop for hanging on
coat hangers in the wardrobe.

Lavender Bag

Stars are frequently found in patchwork, and the LeMoyne Star is a popular pattern. To achieve this tricky eight-seam join, which meets in the center of the star, work slowly and carefully.

MATERIALS

tracing paper and pencil
thin cardboard
utility knife
scraps of silk organza in 3 colors
rotary cutter (optional)
scrap of lining silk
dressmaker's pins
sewing machine and matching thread
iron
needle and matching thread
dried lavender
ribbon

LeMoyne Star

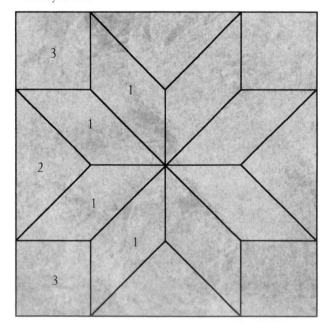

1

Trace the star and make the templates. For each star (you will need 2) cut out 8 pieces from template 1 in 2 colors and 4 pieces each from templates 2 and 3 in the third color. Use a rotary cutter if you wish.

2

To make the star, with right sides facing, pin together 2 piece ones that are in different colors, and stitch them together. Make another pair to match. Press the seams flat but not open, to reduce bulk.

3

Join the 2 pairs together, carefully matching the center seams, pin and stitch. Press the seams flat. Make the other half of the star in the same way.

4

To set in a square 3, swivel the square to match the corner points and pin to the angled edge. To set in a triangle 2, match the corner points and pin to the angled edge. Stitch and press.

5

Set in 3 more triangles to make the patch. Make a second patch in the same way. Measure one side and cut 2 pieces of organza to this length but 2 inches wide. Stitch one to the top of each patch and press. With the right sides facing, stitch around the base and sides of the bag and turn through. Fold a ½-inch hem around the top of the bag, press and top stitch. Fill the bag with dried lavender and tie with a ribbon bow.

Little House Key Ring

Keep your keys safe on this pretty key ring. The little house is made from tiny patched pieces that are appliquéd onto the fob.

MATERIALS

tracing paper, paper and pencil
dressmaker's scissors
red and blue gingham and red fabric scraps
needle and basting thread
iron
cream cotton fabric,
4 × 13 inches
batting
4 × 6 inches
red, cream and blue thread
key ring

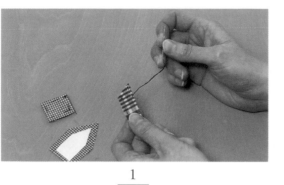

1

Trace the design onto paper and cut out 2 windows, 2 walls, 2 chimneys, a roof and a door. Cut out in scraps of fabric with a ¼-inch seam allowance. Baste to the backing papers and press.

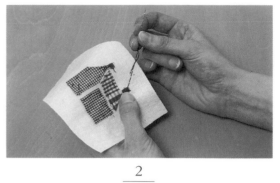

2

Cut 2 main pieces from cream cotton fabric and 2 from batting. Baste the house in sections to one piece of cotton fabric, removing the paper as you go. Slip-stitch the pieces in position with matching thread.

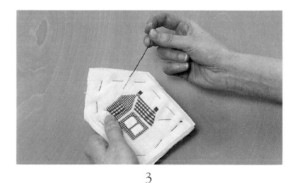

3

Sandwich the batting between the appliquéd and plain fabrics, and baste through all the layers to secure.

4

Cut 3 bias strips in gingham. Press under ¼-inch turnings and bind the raw edges leaving 1 inch free on either side of the point. Thread the ends through the key ring and slip-stitch together.

Key fob and motif template

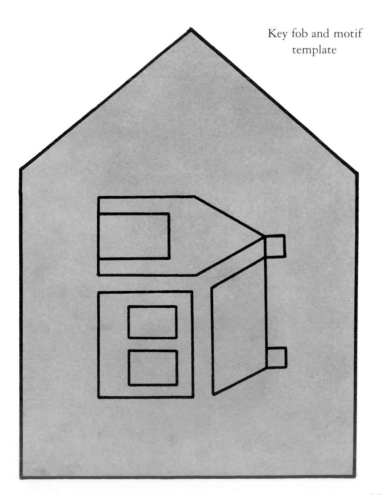

Patchwork Cards

Patchwork designs like this Northumberland star can be used to make unusual gift cards. Work out a design on paper and trace the design onto the bonding web.

*tracing paper and pencil
ruler
iron-on fusible bonding
web
iron
assortment of fabric scraps
dressmaker's scissors
colored cardboard
metallic marker*

1

Cut out the shapes. Iron the shapes onto the back of the fabric scraps and cut out without a seam allowance.

2

Lay the shapes on the cardboard to make up the design. Cover with a clean cloth and iron. Outline the design with the marker.

Photo Frame

Blue and white checked fabrics make a fresh-looking border for a favorite photo.

Cut out a center square from one piece of the cardboard, leaving a 2-inch border. Cut 4 gingham border strips 11 × 4 inches. Cut 3-inch squares of cream-colored fabric and press under the raw edges to make 2-inch squares. Iron bonding web to the reverse of the fabric scraps and cut out 4 flower shapes and 4 pairs of leaves.

MATERIALS

*2 pieces of thick cardboard,
8-inches square
utility knife
scraps of blue and white
gingham and checked
fabric
dressmaker's scissors
scraps of cream-colored fabric
iron
iron-on fusible bonding
web
assorted scraps of fabric for
the flowers
green and navy embroidery
floss
crewel needle
dressmaker's pins
needle and matching
thread
fabric glue
double-sided tape*

1

Pull off the backing from the bonding web and iron a flower and leaves motif to the corner of each cream-colored square, as shown. Embroider the stems in green floss. Cut 4 narrow strips of checked fabric 11 inches long and press under the long edges. Pin and stitch along the center of the gingham borders.

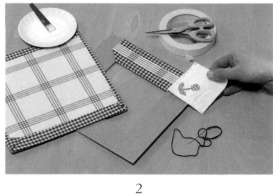

2

Glue the cream-colored squares to the corners of the frame, with the flowers facing outward. Work large stab stitches around the squares in navy thread. Fold the border fabric to the back of the frame and secure with tape. Cover the other piece of cardboard with fabric, then slip-stitch the 2 pieces together around 3 sides, leaving one side open.

Gift Tag

This gift tag would also look very pretty hanging from the closet door key.

MATERIALS

*3-inch square of
18-count Rustico, Zweigart
E3292
stranded cotton DMC nos.
500, 550, 552, 554,
3363, 3364 and 3820
tapestry needle
6-inch square of natural
handmade paper
utility knife
safety ruler
scissors
all-purpose glue
single hole punch
two reinforcing rings*

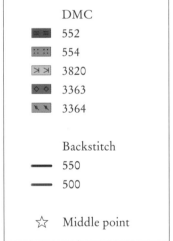

DMC	
▬▬	552
⠸⠿	554
⟩⟩	3820
◆◇	3363
⋉⋉	3364

Backstitch

— 550

— 500

☆ Middle point

1

Beginning in the center of the canvas, work the cross-stitch design using two strands of cotton and the backstitch using a single strand.

2

Cut 2 tag shapes out of the handmade paper, and with the knife, cut an opening in one. Stick the embroidered panel in the window and trim the edges of the fabric. Glue the back of the label in place.

3

Once the glue has dried, punch a hole at the end of the tag and stick the reinforcing rings on either side. Braid a length of dark green, gold and purple thread together and loop them through the hole to finish off the tag.

Greeting Card

1

Baste the fine calico to the back of the silk and fit into a hoop. Baste the waste canvas onto the middle of the fabric, keeping the canvas in line with the grain of the fabric. Mark the center of the canvas. Stitch the design using 2 strands of cotton. When complete, fray and pull out the canvas threads one at a time. Press on the reverse side and trim to fit behind the opening.

2

Stick tape around the inside edge of the opening and position the embroidery on top. Stick the backing cardboard in position. Use double-sided tape to assemble, because glue tends to buckle the cardboard.

MATERIALS

8-inch square of fine calico
8-inch square of
cream-colored silk dupion
(mid-weight silk)
basting thread
needle
embroidery hoop
5 × 6 inches
14-count waste canvas
stranded cotton DMC nos.
221, 223, 224, 744,
3362 and 3363
embroidery needle
scissors
iron
craft card with a
3 × 4¾-inch aperture
double-sided tape

	DMC		
==	224	✕✕	3363
∷∷	223	◢◢	3362
◼▷	221		
◇◇	744	☆	Middle point

Handkerchief Case

No more searching through the drawer – this pretty and practical pouch with its dainty trellis pattern will keep all your hankies tidy.

MATERIALS

*two 21 × 8-inch pieces of
white 36-count evenweave
linen
basting thread
needle
embroidery hoop
stranded cotton DMC nos.
221, 223, 224, 225, 501,
502, 503, 832, 834, 839,
3032 and 3782
tapestry needle
iron
pins
sewing machine
sewing thread
scissors
1 yard wine-colored piping*

1

Baste a guideline horizontally 4 inches from one end of the linen. Mark the center of this line and begin the cross-stitch. The bottom of the design is the side nearest the raw edge.

2

Work the design using a single strand of cotton over 2 threads of linen. When the embroidery is complete, press on the reverse side. A magnifying glass might help.

DMC		DMC	
--	501	5 5	225
1 1	502	7 7	839
1 1	503	9 9	832
2 2	221	II II	834
3 3	223	◇ ◇	3032
4 4	224	x x	3782

☆ Middle point

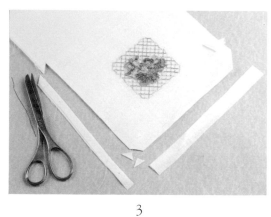

3

Pin the 2 linen panels together with the embroidery to the inside. With a ¼-inch seam allowance, sew all around, leaving a gap on one side for turning. Trim the seams and across the corners, then turn through.

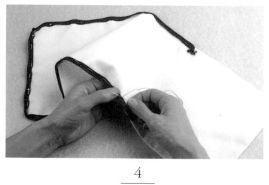

4

Fold the panel in three and baste along the fold lines. Pin the piping to the inside of the front flap and down both sides as far as the second fold line. Turn under the ends and slip-stitch the piping in place. Slip-stitch the side seams to complete the case.

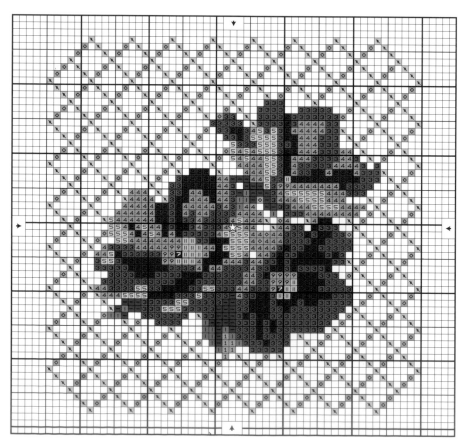

TOKENS TO TREASURE
....

Birth Keepsake

This gift has a practical use as a pincushion but could be filled with lavender instead.

MATERIALS

6-inch square of white 25-count Lugana, Zweigart E3835
basting thread
needle
embroidery hoop
stranded cotton DMC nos. 350, 472 and 3326
tapestry needle
118 small pink beads
scissors
6-inch square of white backing fabric
sewing machine
sewing thread
5 ½-inch squares of batting
pins
30 inches white crocheted lace edging (dipped in weak tea to color slightly)

1

Baste guidelines in both directions across the center of the linen. Work the cross-stitch using 3 strands of cotton over 2 threads. Once complete, sew a bead over the top of each stitch in the pink hearts. Use a double length of thread and begin with a secure knot.

DMC		
▽ ▽ ▽	350	☆ Middle point
△ △ △	472	
◆ ◆ ◆	3326	

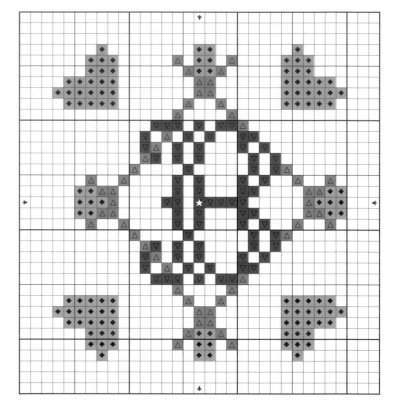

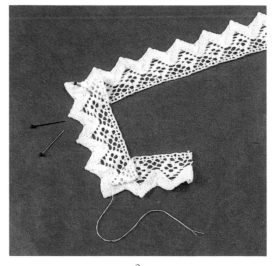

2

Block the design if necessary and trim away the excess fabric, leaving 1½ inches around the cross-stitch. Cut the backing fabric to match and stitch the embroidery and backing fabric together, with right sides facing, leaving a gap along one side. Trim the seams and across the corners to reduce bulk.

3

Tuck the batting into the cushion and slip-stitch to close. Miter the corners of the lace one at a time by folding and stitching diagonally on the wrong side. Each side should be about 5 inches long. Join the lace ends and pin around the cushion ½ inch in from the edge. Stitch neatly in place.

Baby Birth Gift

Celebrate a baby's birth by giving the parents this very pretty arrangement in an unusual but practical container. The display incorporates double tulips, ranunculus, phlox and spray roses, with small leaves of pittosporum.

The choice of soft, subtle colors means that the arrangement is suitable for either a boy or a girl. There is also the added bonus of the beautiful scents of the phlox and dried lavender. Since the arrangement has its own container, it is particularly convenient for a recipient in the hospital, avoiding, as it does, the need to find a vase. Finally, the container can be kept and used again after the life of the display.

MATERIALS

block plastic foam
scissors
small galvanized metal bucket
bunch of pittosporum
15 stems pale pink 'Angelique' tulips
5 stems white spray roses
10 stems white ranunculus
10 stems white phlox
bunch of dried lavender
purple and white check ribbon

1

Soak the plastic foam in water, cut it to fit the small metal bucket and wedge it firmly in place. Cut the pittosporum to a length of 4¾ inches and clean the leaves from the lower part of the stems. Push the stems into the plastic foam to create an overall domed foliage outline within which the flowers can be arranged.

2

Cut the 'Angelique' tulips to a stem length of 4 inches and distribute them evenly throughout the foliage. Cut individual offshoots from the main stems of the spray roses to a length of 4 inches, and arrange throughout the display, with full blooms at the center and buds around the outside.

3

Cut the ranunculus and phlox to a stem length of 4 inches and distribute both throughout the display. Cut the lavender to a stem length of 4¾ inches and arrange in groups of 3 stems evenly throughout the flowers and foliage. Tie the ribbon around the bucket and finish in a generous bow.

Planted Basket for Baby

This display of potted plants in a basket makes a lovely gift to celebrate the birth of a baby. It is easy to make and is a long-lasting alternative to a cut-flower arrangement.

The combination of two simple and delicate white plants, baby cyclamen and lily of the valley, gives the design charm and purity; indeed, everything about it says "baby."

MATERIALS

wire basket
2 handfuls Spanish moss
cellophane
scissors
3 pots miniature white cyclamen
3 pots lily of the valley
paper ribbon

1

Line the wire basket with generous handfuls of Spanish moss, then carefully line the moss with cellophane. Trim the cellophane so that it fits neatly around the rim of the basket.

2

Remove the plants from their pots carefully. Loosen the soil and the roots a little before planting them in the basket, alternating the cyclamen with the lily of the valley and adding more moss if necessary.

3

Make sure that the plants are firmly bedded in the basket. Make two small bows from the paper ribbon, smoothing open the ends, and attach one to each side of the basket at the base of the handle.

Herb Bath-sachet

Enjoy a traditional herbal bath by filling a fine muslin bag with relaxing herbs, tying it to the faucet and letting the hot water run through. This drawstring design means it can be reused time after time if you keep refilling it with new herbs. Chamomile and hops are relaxing; basil, bay, mint, lemon balm and sage are invigorating.

MATERIALS

silky muslin, about 12 × 16 in
pins, needle and thread

scissors
fabric scraps, for casing
39 in narrow ribbon

safety pin
herbal bath-mix or any combination of dried herbs

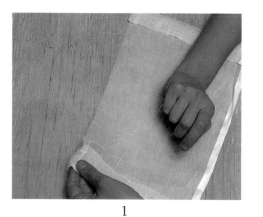

1

With right sides facing, fold over about 2 in of the silky muslin at both short ends, pin and stitch each side. Trim the seams. Turn right-side out.

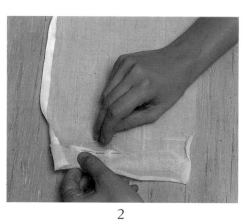

2

Turn in and hem the raw edges of the folded-over ends.

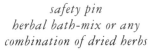

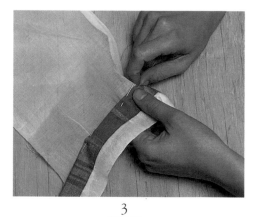

3

Cut two strips of cotton fabric about 1 in wide and as long as the width of the muslin, with about ¼ in extra for turnings all round. Iron a hem along both long edges. Turn in and hem the ends, then pin one casing on the right side of the muslin so the bottom edge of the casing lines up with the hem line. Neatly stitch the casing in place along both long seams. Repeat with the other casing.

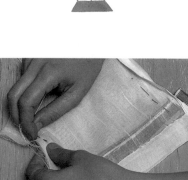

4

With right sides together, fold the muslin in half so the casings line up. Stitch the side seams from the bottom edge of the casing to the bottom edge of the bag. Trim the seams.

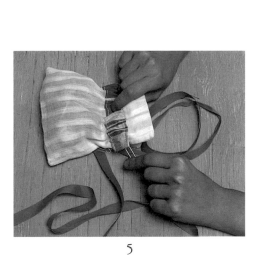

_5_

Cut the ribbon in half, attach a safety pin to one end and use this to thread the ribbon through the casing so both ends finish up at the same side. Remove the safety pin.

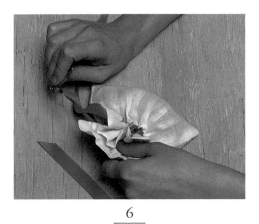

_6_

Attach the safety pin to one end of the other piece of ribbon and thread it through the casing in the other direction so the ends finish up at the other side. Fill with herbs ready for use.

Shell Pot

Decorate a flowerpot with shells and some old netting, and then use it to hold plants, pencils, paintbrushes, strings, ribbon, or any paraphernalia that needs to be kept in check. It's a pretty and inexpensive way to make a very special container.

MATERIALS

small net bag
flowerpot, 7 in tall
scissors
hot glue gun and glue sticks
thick string
small cowrie shells
cockle shells
starfish or similar central motif

1

Slip the net bag over the flowerpot and trim the top edge. Secure it by gluing on a length of string.

2

Using a glue gun, position a row of cowrie shells along the top edge.

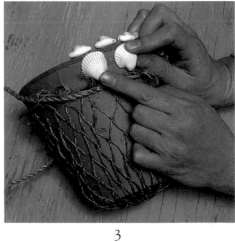

3

Glue cockle shells around the rim; position the starfish and four cockle shells in the front.

Shell Box

A simple cardboard box takes on a South Seas feel when decorated with half-cowries. Available from craft shops, their flattened bottoms make them easy to stick to surfaces. Here, some have also been strung together to make a toggle for fastening.

MATERIALS

hot glue gun and glue sticks
raffia
small cardboard box
half-cowrie shells
upholstery needle

1

Glue a loop of raffia from the bottom of the box, up the back and along the top.

2

Tie half-cowries into a bunch on a length of raffia, tying each one in separately. Leave a short length of raffia free. Pierce the front of the box with an upholstery needle and thread the raffia through. Knot it on the inside.

3

Glue on a pattern of half-cowries to decorate the outside of the box.

Shell Candle Centerpiece

An old flowerpot, scallop shells salvaged from the fish market and smaller shells picked up from the beach make up a fabulous centerpiece. Put a candle in the center or fill it with dried fruits or flowers.

MATERIALS

hot glue gun and glue sticks
8 curved scallop shells
flowerpot, 7 in tall
bag of cockle shells
4 flat scallop shells
newspaper, florist's foam or
other packing material
saucer
candle
raffia

1

Generously apply hot glue to the inside lower edge of a large curved scallop shell. Hold it in place on the rim of the pot for a few seconds until it is firmly stuck. Continue sticking shells to the top of the pot, arranging them so they overlap slightly, until the whole of the rim has been covered.

2

In the same way, glue a cockle shell where two scallops join. Continue all around the pot.

3

Place another row of cockles at the joins of the first row. Glue flat scallop shells face upwards to the bottom of the pot, first at the front, then at the back, and then the two sides, to ensure the pot stands straight.

4

Fill the pot with packing material and place a saucer on top of this. Stand a candle on the saucer.

5

Tie raffia around the pot where it joins the stand.

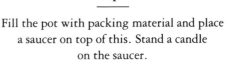

6

Decorate the stand with a few more cockles, if you like. Stand a few more curved scallop shells inside the original row to create a fuller, more petalled shape.

Shell Mirror

The subtle rose-pinks of ordinary scallop shells, picked up from the fish market,
make for an easy, eye-catching mirror frame. Here, four large shells
have been used at the corners with smaller ones filling in the sides.

MATERIALS

sandpaper
mirror in wooden frame
paint
paintbrush
4 large flat scallop shells
hot glue gun and glue sticks
10 small flat scallop shells
seagrass string
2 metal eyelets

1

Sand down and paint the mirror frame with
the color of your choice.

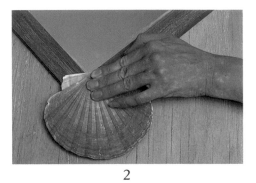

2

Position the large scallop shells at the corners
of the mirror, using the hot glue.

3

In the same way, glue three of the smaller
scallop shells to each side of the mirror.

4

Attach two of the smaller scallop shells to the
top of the mirror and two to the bottom.

5

Braid three lengths of seagrass string
to make a hanger.

6

Screw metal eyelets into each side of the
frame at the back, and tie the hanger
on to these.

Filigree Leaf Wrap

Even the most basic brown wrapping paper can take on a very special look. Use a gilded skeletonized leaf and gold twine in combination with brown paper: coarser string would give a more robust look.

MATERIALS

*Treasure Gold®
large skeletonized leaf
brown paper
sticky tape
gold twine
hot glue gun and glue sticks,
if necessary*

1

Rub Treasure Gold® into the skeletonized leaf.

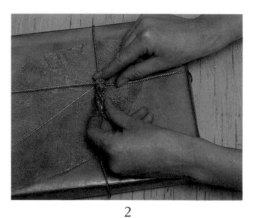

2

Wrap the parcel in the brown paper and rub Treasure Gold® on to the corners. Tie the parcel with gold twine, bringing the two ends together and tying a knot. Fray the ends to create a tassle effect. Slip the leaf under the twine, securing it with glue at each end if necessary.

Fruit and Foliage Gift Wraps

Here, gilded brown parcel paper provides a fitting background for a decoration of leaves and dried fruit slices.

MATERIALS

*brown paper
sticky tape
Treasure Gold®
seagrass string
hot glue gun and glue sticks
dried fruit slices
preserved leaves*

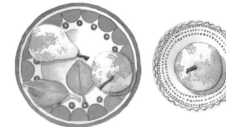

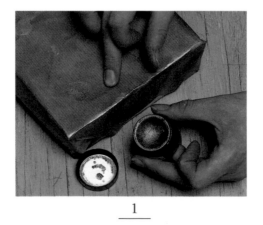

1

Wrap the package with brown paper and rub in Treasure Gold®, paying special attention to the corners.

2

Tie the parcel with seagrass string, and then glue a different dried fruit or leaf to each quarter.

Tissue Rosette Gift Wrap

Tissue papers make a fabulous foundation for any gift-wrapping; they come in a glorious array of colors, and they softly take to any shape.

MATERIALS

*tissue paper in 2 shades
coordinating twine*

1

Place a cylindrical gift in the center of two squares of tissue, one laid on top of the other. Gather the tissue up and tie it with twine.

2

Gently open out the rosette at the top.

Lavender Tissue Gift Wrap

Bunches of lavender add a real country touch to tissue gift wrap, and become part of the gift.

MATERIALS

*dried lavender
twine
tissue paper in 2 shades
sticky tape
glue*

1

Make two bunches of lavender and tie them with twine to form a cross.

2

Wrap the package in the darker toned tissue paper, and then wrap it with the paler tissue, cut to form an envelope. Glue the lavender to the front of the package.

Dried Flower Gift Wrap

To make a present extra special, why not make the wrapping part of the gift? The display is effectively a dried flower corsage but is used to embellish gift wrapping.

It takes a little time to produce but its natural, warm, earthy colors make this a delightful enhancement well worth the effort, and something to keep.

MATERIALS

*dried sunflower head
scissors
florist's wires
small dried pomegranate
3 small pieces dried fungi
(graded in size)
3 slices dried orange
(graded in size)
silver florist's wires
florist's tape
gift-wrapped present
raffia*

1

Cut the sunflower to a stem length of 1 inch and double leg mount on a stub wire. Single leg mount the pomegranates on wire. Double leg mount the small pieces of fungi on wires and mount the orange slices on silver wires.

2

Wrap all the wired materials with tape, then attach the 3 orange slices to one side of the sunflower and pomegranate, then attach the 3 layers of fungi on the other side. Bind all these in place using the silver wire or reel wire, if you prefer.

3

Trim the wire stems to a length of 2 inches and tape together with florist's tape. Tie the raffia around the present and push the wired stem of the decoration under the raffia knot. Secure in place with another wire or pieces of double-sided tape.

Dried Flowers as a Gift

This is a great way to present dried flowers as a gift. Treat them as you would a tied bouquet of cut fresh flowers, prettily wrapped in tissue paper and tied with a large bow.

The deep pink mixture of exotic and garden flowers – protea and amaranthus with peonies and larkspur – makes this a floral gift anyone would be thrilled to receive.

MATERIALS

10 small dried pink
Protea compacta *buds*
10 stems dried pink larkspur
10 stems dried pink peonies
10 stems dried green amaranthus
raffia
scissors
2 sheets blue tissue paper
pink ribbon

1

Lay out the dried materials so that they are all easily accessible. Start the bouquet with a dried protea held in your hand, and add a stem of larkspur, a stem of peony and a stem of amaranthus, turning the bunch with every addition.

2

Continue until all the dried materials have been used. Tie with raffia at the binding point – where the stems cross each other. Trim the stem ends so that their length is approximately one-third of the overall height of the finished bouquet.

3

Lay the sheets of tissue paper on a flat surface and place the bouquet diagonally across the tissue. Wrap the tissue paper around the flowers, overlapping it at the front. Tie securely at the binding point with a ribbon and form a large, floppy bow.

Leafy Pictures

Delicate skeletonized leaves come in such breathtakingly exquisite forms that
they deserve to be shown off. Mount them on handmade papers and frame them
to make simple yet stunning natural collages.

MATERIALS

wooden picture frame
sandpaper
paint
paintbrush
backing paper
pencil
scissors
skeletonized leaf
Treasure Gold®
hot glue gun and glue sticks
mounting paper

1

Take the frame apart and sand it down to
provide a base before painting. A translucent
colorwash has been used for painting here,
but any paint will do.

2

Allow the paint to dry, then sand the
paint back so you're left with a wooden frame
with shading in the moldings, plus a
veil of color on the surface.

3

Use the back of the frame as a template for
the backing paper. Draw around it with a
pencil to form a cutting line.

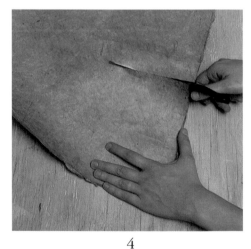

4

Cut the backing paper out.

<u>5</u>

Prepare the leaf by rubbing with Treasure
Gold®. This does take a little time as the gilt
has to be well worked in.

<u>6</u>

Stick the backing paper on the frame back,
glue the mounting paper in the center and
attach the leaf on to that. Here, the leaf is
centered with the stalk breaking the edge of
the mounting paper. Finally, put the
frame back together.

Spicy Pomander

Pomanders were originally nature's own air fresheners. The traditional orange pomanders are fairly tricky to do, because the critical drying process can so easily go wrong, leading to moldy oranges. This one, made of cloves and cardamom pods, offers none of those problems, and makes a refreshing change in soft muted colors.

MATERIALS

*cloves
florist's dry foam ball,
about 3 in diameter
hot glue gun and glue sticks
green cardamom pods
raffia
florist's stub wire*

1

Start by making a single line of cloves all around the circumference of the ball. Make another one in the other direction, so you have divided the ball into quarters.

2

Make a line of cloves on both sides of the original lines to make broad bands of cloves quartering the ball.

3

Starting at the top of the first quarter, glue cardamom pods over the foam, methodically working in rows to create a neat effect. Repeat on the other three quarters.

4

Tie a bow in the center of a length of raffia. Pass a stub wire through the knot and twist the ends together.

5

Attach the bow to the top of the ball
using the stub wire.

6

Join the two loose ends in a knot
for hanging the pomander.

Tulip Pomander

In Elizabethan times pomanders were filled with herbs or scented flowers and were carried to perfume the air. Today the pomander is more likely to be a bridesmaid's accessory.

The pomander illustrated does not boast exotic aromas but it does have a pleasing variety of surface textures, ranging from the spiky inner petals of double tulips through the beady black berries of myrtle to the softness of gray moss, all set against bands of smooth satin ribbon. It would be a charming alternative to the bridesmaid's traditional posy.

MATERIALS

*plastic foam ball
ribbon
scissors
20 heads 'Appleblossom'
double tulips
bunch myrtle
florist's wires
good handful of
reindeer moss*

1

Soak the foam ball in water. Tie the ribbon around the ball, starting at the top and crossing at the bottom, and then tying at the top to divide the ball into four equal segments. Make sure there is enough ribbon to tie into a bow.

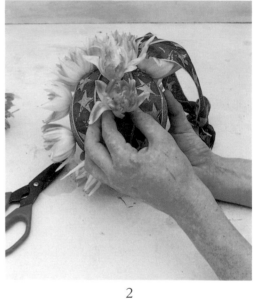

2

Cut the tulips to a stem length of about 1 inch and push into the foam in vertical lines at the center of each segment. Hold the tulip heads gently while positioning them on the foam ball to prevent the heads from breaking off.

3

Push sprigs of myrtle into the foam to form lines on either side of each line of tulips.

4

Use bent wires to cover all remaining exposed areas of the foam ball with moss.

Cinnamon and Orange Ring

The warm colors, spicy smell and culinary content of this small decorated ring make it perfect for the wall of a kitchen. The display is not complicated to make but requires nimble fingers to handle the very small pieces of cinnamon used. These pieces have to be tightly packed together to achieve the right effect, and attaching so much cinnamon to the plastic foam may cause it to collapse. To prevent this from happening, you can glue the foam ring to a piece of cardboard cut to the same outline before you begin.

MATERIALS

glue gun and glue sticks
5 dried oranges
plastic foam ring for
dried flowers,
5¾ inches in diameter
20 cinnamon sticks

1

Apply glue to the bases of the dried oranges and space them evenly around the foam ring. Break the cinnamon sticks into ¾–1½-inch pieces.

2

Apply glue to the bottom of the pieces of cinnamon and push them into the foam between the dried oranges, keeping them close together.

3

Glue a line of the cinnamon pieces around both the inside and outside edges of the ring to cover the plastic foam completely.

Classic Orange and Clove Pomander

This classic pomander starts as fresh material that, as you use it, dries into a beautiful old-fashioned decoration with a warm, spicy smell evocative of mulled wine and the festive season. Make several pomanders using different ribbons and display them in a bowl, hang them around the house, use them as Christmas decorations or even hang them in the linen closet to perfume your sheets and towels.

MATERIALS

3 small firm oranges
3 types of ribbon
scissors
cloves

1	2	3
Tie a ribbon around an orange, crossing it over at the base so that it neatly quarters the orange.	Finish off at the top of the orange by tying the ribbon into a bow. Clip the ends of the ribbon to prevent it from fraying.	Starting at the edges of the areas, push the sharp ends of the exposed cloves into the orange and continue until it is completely covered.

Red Tied Sheaf

A tied sheaf of flowers arranged in the hand makes an attractive and informal wall decoration. To make a successful wall hanging, the sheaf must be made with a flat back, while at the same time it should have a profiled front to add visual interest. This richly colored display would make a wonderful housewarming gift.

The demanding aspect of the construction of the sheaf is the technique of spiraling the materials in your hand. But this display is relatively small, which simplifies the task.

MATERIALS

50 stems dried lavender
10 stems Protea compacta *buds*
10 stems natural ti tree
15 stems dried red roses
twine
scissors
satin ribbon, 2 inches wide

1

Lay out the materials so that they are easily accessible and separate the lavender into 10 smaller groups. Hold the longest protea in your hand, and behind it add a slightly longer stem of ti tree, then hold rose stems to either side of the protea, both slightly shorter than the first. Continue adding materials in a regular repeating sequence to the growing bunch in your hand, spiraling the stems as you do so.

2

When all the materials have been used, tie the sheath with twine at the binding point. Trim the stems so that they make up about one-third of the overall length of the sheaf.

3

To finish the display make a separate ribbon bow and attach it to the sheaf at the binding point.

Rose and Clove Pomander

This pomander is a decadent display of rose heads massed in a ball. But it has a secret: cloves hidden between the rose heads, giving the pomander its lasting spicy perfume. It relies for its impact on the use of large quantities of tightly packed flowers, all of the same type and color.

Almost profligate in its use of materials, this pomander is quick to make and would be a wonderful and very special gift.

1

Fold the ribbon in half and double leg mount its cut ends together with a wire. To form a ribbon handle, push the wires right through the plastic foam ball so that they come out the other end, and pull the projecting wires so that the double leg mounted part of the ribbon becomes firmly embedded in the plastic foam. Turn the excess wire back into the foam.

MATERIALS

ribbon, 16 × 1 inch
florist's wire
plastic foam ball for dried
flowers, approximately
4 inches in diameter
scissors
100 stems dried roses
200 cloves

2

Cut the stems of the dried rose heads to a length of approximately 1 inch. Starting at the top of the plastic foam ball, push the stems of the dried rose heads into the foam to form a tightly packed circle around the base of the ribbon handle. As you work, push a clove into the plastic foam between each rose head. Continue forming concentric circles of rose heads and cloves around the plastic foam ball until it is completely covered.

Herbal Centerpiece

Extremely strong-smelling herbs should be avoided for table centerpieces because their fragrance may overpower the meal. However, gently scented herbs make a delightful table decoration.

MATERIALS

*shallow basket without handle
2 blocks florist's foam for dried
flowers
2 bunches cardoon thistles
florist's wire
florist's tape
scissors
3 large ivory candles
bunches of dried herbs, where
possible in flower, including lavender,
marjoram and fennel*

Caution Make sure that this arrangement is never left unattended while the candles are lit.

1

Fill the basket with foam, wedging it into position. Group the cardoon heads into 3 positions in the foam. Make hairpins from lengths of wire, and tape 3 hairpins around the base of each candle. Place the candles into the foam.

2

Wire small bunches of lavender and marjoram, and spread evenly around the arrangement. Place the fennel flower heads in the arrangement singly or wired together in groups, depending upon the space you wish to fill.

Dried Herbal Topiary Tree

Topiary trees are an attractive way of displaying flowers and natural objects. This design includes small terra-cotta pots, which add to the textural interest in the top of the tree.

MATERIALS

large terra-cotta pot for the base
cement or plaster of Paris
piece of tree branch for the trunk
5-inch ball of florist's foam for dried flowers
small pieces of similar foam
2 large bunches of glycerined copper beech foliage or other preserved foliage
scissors
heavy-gauge florist's wire
wire cutters
12 miniature terra-cotta pots
2 bunches goldenrod
light florist's wire
hot glue gun (optional)
2 bunches poppy heads

1

Cover the hole in the large terra-cotta pot and half fill with wet cement or plaster of Paris. As the cement begins to harden, stand the branch in the pot to form the trunk. Let dry for at least 48 hours before proceeding to the next step.

2

Press the foam ball onto the trunk, making sure it is firmly in place, but not so far down that the trunk comes out the other side of the ball. Cover the cement in the base with pieces of foam.

3

Cover the ball and base with pieces of copper beech or other preserved foliage. Thread heavy-gauge wire through the holes in the small pots and make a stem so they can be attached to the tree and pressed into the foam.

4

Arrange the pots through the tree and base, and fill with small wired bunches of goldenrod, trimming with scissors where needed. These can be glued into position if necessary. Finally, add the poppy heads.

Herbal Christmas Wreath

Orange slices can be dried on a wire rack in an oven at the lowest possible setting for several hours until they are crisp. They should then be carefully varnished with a clear, matte varnish so that they cannot reabsorb moisture from the atmosphere.

MATERIALS

few stems fresh holly
2 sprays fresh conifer
scissors
hot glue gun
wreath ring, approximately
9 inches in diameter
gold spray paint
2-inch terra-cotta pot
broken pieces of terra-cotta pot
7 ears of wheat, sprayed gold
small bunch of dried sage
small bunch of oregano
florist's wire
3 dried orange slices

1

Attach the holly and conifer to the ring using the hot glue gun. Cover approximately half the ring.

2

In a well-ventilated area, spray a little gold paint onto the pot and pieces of pot and glue them to the design. Add the ears of wheat. Make small bunches of sage and tuck them among the pieces of broken pot.

3

Make a chunky bunch of the dried oregano, wiring it together. Glue into the main pot in the center of the design. Cut the orange slices into quarters and glue those into the arrangement. The fresh ingredients will dry on the wreath and look most attractive.

Dried Herbal Posy

This posy could be given as a present or to say thank you. It would also make a very pretty dressing-table decoration. The ingredients are dried, so it can be made well in advance or you could make a few to have ready to give to guests.

MATERIALS

small bunch dried red roses
florist's wire
small bunch alchemilla
small bunch marjoram
cotton posy frill, deep pink
3 sprays dried bay leaves
hot glue gun
florist's tape
scissors
ribbon, as desired

1

Start with a small cluster of red roses, binding them with wire to form a center. Add some alchemilla, binding gently but firmly in the same spot.

2

Bind in some marjoram and then more red roses and alchemilla, until you are happy with the size of the posy. Carefully push the stems of the paper posy through the center of the posy frill.

3

Separate the bay leaves from the stems and glue them in, one at a time, through the arrangement and around the edge as a border.

4

Push the posy frill up toward the flowers and fasten with tape. Tie ribbon around the stem of the posy and make a bow.

Bath Bags

These are much more fun than putting commercial bubble bath in the water. Tie them over the faucet and make sure the hot water is running through them — this will release lovely herbal scents that relax and comfort you.

9-inch-diameter circles of muslin
6 tablespoons bran
1 tablespoon lavender flowers
1 tablespoon chamomile flowers
1 tablespoon rosemary tips
3 small rubber bands
3 yards narrow ribbon or twine

1

Place 2 tablespoons bran in the center of each circle of muslin. Add the lavender to one bag, the chamomile to a second and the rosemary to the third, mixing the herbs through the bran.

2

Gather each circle of material up and close with a rubber band. Then tie a length of ribbon or twine around each bag to make a loop so that the bag can be hung from the hot-water faucet in the stream of water.

Herb Corsages

Making your own boutonniere or corsage is easy. Tiny posy frills are obtainable from floral suppliers or you could use the center of a small paper doily.

MATERIALS

*medium-sized flower
sprig of any herb with attractive
leaves
thin florist's wire
miniature posy frill or cut-down
doily
florist's tape*

1

For a centerpiece, you could use a rose or small spray carnation. wrap some herb foliage around it – fresh green parsley would look good – and then bind it tightly with thin wire.

2

Push the stems through the center of the frill and tape them together, covering the stems all the way down. Other combinations could include rosemary, sage, lavender or box.

Scented Valentine Heart

Valentine gifts in the shape of a heart are always popular. This heart-shaped gift box with dried flower and herb decoration on the lid is accompanied by a matching wreath made with fresh leaves and flowers that remain attractive when they dry.

MATERIALS

heart-shaped box
broad and narrow ribbon
hot glue gun
5 dried roses
dried bay leaves
bunch of dried goldenrod
heart-shaped wreath form
houttuynia leaves
'Minuet' roses
sprig of fresh lavender

1

Start decorating the gift box by making a large bow with broad ribbon. Then glue the dried ingredients onto the box to resemble a bunch of flowers. Stick the bow on top.

2

Wrap some narrow ribbon around the wreath form and secure with glue. Add a few houttuynia leaves (this variety is *H. cordata*), some 'Minuet' roses and fresh lavender. These could be attached with wire instead of glue if you prefer.

Herb-decorated Crackers

Homemade touches are important at Christmas, as they add the final touch to a family celebration. These crackers are easy to decorate and could be made by adults and children together. Buy ready-decorated crackers and remove the commercial trimming.

MATERIALS

crackers
narrow ribbon, as desired
scissors
small sprigs of various herbs, pretzels,
gilded rosehips
hot glue gun or general-purpose
adhesive

1

Tie the ends of the crackers with ribbon, making attractive bows.

2

Make small posies of herbs and glue them to the central part of the crackers. Add pretzels and gilded rosehips.

Scented Pressed Herb Diary

A notebook or diary can be scented by placing it in a box with a strong lavender sachet or a cotton ball sprinkled with a few drops of essential oil. Leave it in the sealed box for a month or so to impart a sweet, lingering fragrance. Try to find a very plain diary or notebook that does not have lettering or decoration on the cover, as these would spoil the design. Use a sheet of plastic wrapping paper made for covering books.

MATERIALS

*pressed leaves and flowers, such as
borage flowers, alchemilla flowers
and small leaves, daisies, single roses
and forget-me-nots
plain diary or notebook
tweezers
large tapestry needle
white latex adhesive
clear plastic wrapping paper
iron and cloth pad (optional)*

1

Start by arranging a selection of pressed leaves on the front of the diary or notebook, using the tweezers for positioning.

2

Continue to build up your design by adding the pressed flowerheads.

3

Once you are happy with the design, stick it down, using a large tapestry needle and latex adhesive. Slide the needle into the glue and then, without moving the design, place a small amount of glue under each leaf and petal so that they are secure. Cover with clear plastic wrapping paper. Some kinds of plastic wrapping paper need heating, and you should iron gently with a cloth pad between the film and the iron.

Pressed Herb Cards

A homemade card is one that will always be treasured long after the occasion has passed. Although it takes time and trouble to make your own cards, it is always worth the effort to give someone something with your personal touch.

MATERIALS

*pressed herbs and flowers, such as
blue cornflower, ivy, rosemary and
borage
blank greeting card
tweezers
large tapestry needle
white latex adhesive
clear plastic film
iron and cloth pad (optional)*

1

Arrange a selection of pressed herbs and flowers on the front of the card, using tweezers to position them.

2

When the design is complete, stick it down using a tapestry needle to slide dabs of adhesive beneath the herbs and flowers without altering their position. Cover with a sheet of plastic wrapping paper. If the plastic needs heating, iron with a cloth pad between the plastic and the iron.

Bath-lotion Bottle

Recycle a glass bottle containing homemade lotion and decorate it with corrugated cardboard in gem-like colors for a real impact.

MATERIALS

*scissors
colored corrugated cardboard
flower water bottle
hot glue gun and glue sticks
colored raffia*

1

Cut the corrugated cardboard to size, and then glue in position around the bottle. Tie with raffia.

2

Make a matching label from corrugated cardboard, and tie it on using raffia.

Bath-lotion Jar

Decorate a jar of lotion to complement the bottle, using brilliantly colored fine corrugated cardboard. Royal blue and emerald green make a rich combination that could be used for both men and women.

MATERIALS

*scissors
colored corrugated cardboard
baby food jar
hot glue gun and glue sticks
twine*

1

Cut the corrugated cardboard to size, and then glue in place around the jar. Tie the twine around the jar.

2

Cut a piece of corrugated cardboard to fit the top of the lid and glue it in place. Glue twine to cover the side of the lid.

TOKENS TO TREASURE

Chamomile and Honey Mask

Although this mask makes you look a little strange while it is on your face, it smooths and softens skin beautifully. Chamomile flowers are usually easy to obtain at health food stores as they are often used for making chamomile tea.

INGREDIENTS

1 tablespoon dried chamomile flowers
6 fluid ounces boiling water
2 tablespoons bran
1 teaspoon honey, warmed

1

Pour the boiling water over the chamomile flowers and let them stand for 30 minutes. Then strain the infusion and discard the chamomile flowers.

2

Mix 3 tablespoons of the liquid with the bran and honey and rub this mixture over your face. Set aside for at least 10 minutes, then rinse off with warm water.

Tansy Skin Tonic

Tansy leaves smell fairly strong, but this tonic will invigorate your skin, especially if you keep the bottle in the refrigerator. Splash on this cool herbal liquid to start the day.

INGREDIENTS

large handful tansy leaves
⅔ cup water
⅔ cup milk
bottle for storing

1

Put the leaves, water and milk in a small pan and bring to a boil. Simmer for 15 minutes, then let cool in the pan.

2

Strain the tonic into a bottle. Keep the mixture in the refrigerator, and apply cold to the skin as a soothing toner or tonic.

Feverfew Complexion Milk

Feverfew grows prolifically in the garden, self-seeding all over the herb beds, and this is a welcome use for this overenthusiastic plant. The milk will moisturize dry skin, help to fade blemishes and discourage blackheads.

Feverfew can be cultivated easily; it is especially pretty grown in tubs and pots in the greenhouse or conservatory.

Hang bunches of flowers upside down and let air dry; use as a decorative addition to dried flower arrangements.

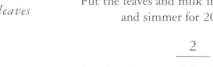

INGREDIENTS

large handful of feverfew leaves
1⅓ cup milk
bottle for storing

1

Put the leaves and milk in a small saucepan and simmer for 20 minutes.

2

Let the mixture cool in the pan, then strain into a bottle. Keep it in the refrigerator.

Fennel Cleanser

Fennel is another herb that self-seeds all over the garden, so once you have planted it supplies will be no problem. The leaves have an aniseed aroma. This mixture gently but thoroughly cleanses the day's grime away.

The tall, graceful heads of fennel seeds add height to a cottage herb garden. The seeds are valued for their distinctive aroma. In Victorian times the seeds came to symbolize the virtue of strength.

At one time, fennel seeds were combined with those of dill and caraway in little sacks or purses, to be chewed at prayer meetings to quell hunger pangs: they were known as "meeting seeds."

INGREDIENTS

1 tablespoon fennel seed
1 cup boiling water
1 teaspoon honey
2 tablespoons buttermilk

1

Lightly crush the fennel seeds, pour the boiling water over them and let infuse for about 30 minutes.

2

Strain the cooled liquid into a small bowl and add the honey and buttermilk. Transfer to a clean bottle and keep the mixture refrigerated.

Parsley Hair Tonic

Parsley stimulates the scalp and gets the circulation going, which aids hair growth and adds shine. Parsley is cultivated in the garden in numerous forms, including curly, plain and turnip-rooted. It is one of the most versatile herbs, and no herb garden should be without at least one plant.

INGREDIENTS

*large handful parsley sprigs
2 tablespoons water*

1

Place the parsley sprigs and water in a food processor.

2

Process until ground to a smooth puree. Apply the green lotion to the scalp, then wrap your head in a warm towel and leave for about 1 hour before shampooing as normal.

Lemon Verbena Hair Rinse

Add a delicious fragrance to your hair with this rinse. It will also stimulate the pores and circulation. Lemon verbena is worth growing in the garden, if only so that you can walk by and pick a wonderfully scented leaf.

INGREDIENTS

*handful lemon verbena leaves
1 cup boiling water*

1

Pour the boiling water over the lemon verbena leaves and let soak for 1 hour.

2

Strain the mixture and discard the leaves. Pour this rinse over your hair after conditioning.

Chamomile Conditioning Rinse

Chamomile flowers help keep blond hair a bright, clear color. They will not lift the color in hair that is medium to dark, but will help brighten naturally fair hair, as well as leaving a pleasant fragrance.

INGREDIENTS

½ cup chamomile flowers
1 pint water
handful of scented geranium leaves
bottle for storing

1

Place the flowers and water in a saucepan and bring to a boil. Simmer for approximately 15 minutes.

2

While the liquid is still hot, strain over the scented geranium leaves. Let soak for 30 to 40 minutes. Strain again, this time into a bottle. Use the mixture after shampooing.

Rosemary Hair Tonic

Rosemary is an excellent substitute for mildly medicated shampoos, and this tonic also helps control greasy hair and enhances the shine and natural color.

INGREDIENTS

1 cup fresh rosemary tips
5 cups bottled water
bottle for storing

1

Put the ingredients in a saucepan and bring to a boil. Simmer for approximately 20 minutes, then let cool in the pan.

2

Strain the mixture and store it in a clean bottle. Use after shampooing.

Dill Aftershave

Most recipes are for fragrances for women, so here is one for men. It is best kept in the refrigerator so that the cool liquid has a bracing effect and smells good.

INGREDIENTS

¼ cup dill seed
1 tablespoon honey
2½ cups bottled water
1 tablespoon distilled witch hazel
bottle for storing

1

Place the dill seed, honey and water in a small saucepan and bring to a boil. Simmer for about 20 minutes.

2

Let cool in the pan, then add the witch hazel. Strain the cooled mixture into a bottle and refrigerate.

Lavender Bubble Bath

There is no need to buy commercially made bubble baths again. This fragrance is quite lovely and so simple to make that you can make some spares as gifts for friends and family—you will be in great demand!

INGREDIENTS

*bunch of lavender
clean wide-necked jar, with screw top
large bottle of clear organic shampoo
5 drops oil of lavender*

1

Place the bunch of lavender head downward in the jar. If the stalks are longer than the jar cut them down, as it is the flowers that do the work. Add the shampoo and the lavender oil.

2

Close the jar and place on a sunny windowsill for 2 to 3 weeks, shaking occasionally.

3

Strain the liquid and rebottle. Use about 1 tablespoon in a bath.

Lemongrass, Coriander and Clove Bath

If you are suffering from stiff limbs after excessive exercise, this bath will help stimulate the circulation and relieve suffering in joints and muscles.

INGREDIENTS

2 tablespoons almond oil
2 drops lemongrass oil
2 drops coriander oil
2 drops clove oil

1

Carefully measure the almond oil into a small dish.

2

Slowly drop in the other essential oils. Mix all the ingredients and pour into the bath while the water is running.

Lavender and Marjoram Bath

This bath mixture has the added bonus of moisturizing the skin while it gently soothes away cares and troubles. The essential oils induce sleep. To enhance the effect, you could add a bath bag containing fresh lavender and marjoram to the water.

Lavender oil is the most useful of all the essential oils, and perhaps the safest. Allergic reaction is virtually unknown and, unlike many of the other essential oils, it is safe to apply it directly to the skin.

It can help to promote sleep – sprinkle a few drops onto the pillow, or onto a handkerchief placed on the pillow, for adults and children to enjoy untroubled rest.

It is also excellent for treating burns, stings, scalds and minor wounds. Deter flying insects by rubbing the essential oil into uncovered parts of the body, such as hands and feet, on a warm evening when sitting outside.

INGREDIENTS

2 tablespoons almond oil
7 drops lavender oil
3 drops marjoram oil

1

Measure out all the ingredients into a small dish or bowl.

2

Combine all the ingredients and pour them into the bath while the water is running, then have a long, soothing soak.

COUNTRY
Cooking

LIZ TRIGG

Spring Recipes

*Spring brings the first of the year's tender young
vegetables, and there are plenty of tempting recipes
to make the most of seasonal produce. Treat yourself
to a zesty lemon cake or an Easter tea studded
with fruit and spices, for an Easter breakfast.*

Warm Chicken Salad with Sesame and Coriander

INGREDIENTS

*4 medium chicken breasts, boned and
skinned
8 ounces snow peas
2 heads decorative lettuce
3 carrots, peeled and julienned
6 ounces button mushrooms, sliced
6 slices of bacon, fried*

*For the dressing
½ cup lemon juice
2 tablespoons whole-grain mustard
1 cup olive oil
5 tablespoons sesame oil
1 teaspoon coriander seeds, crushed
1 tablespoon fresh cilantro leaves
chopped, to garnish*

Serves 6

1

Mix all the dressing ingredients in a bowl.
Place the chicken in a dish and pour on
half the dressing. Refrigerate overnight.

2

Cook the snow peas for 2 minutes in
boiling water, then cool under cold running
water to prevent them from cooking any
more. Tear the lettuces into small pieces,
mix with all the other salad ingredients and
divide among six bowls.

3

Broil the chicken breasts until cooked
through, then slice them on the diagonal
into strips. Divide among the bowls of
salad, and add some dressing to each dish.
Combine quickly and scatter some fresh
cilantro over each bowl.

Spinach and Roquefort Pancakes

INGREDIENTS

*1 cup plain all-purpose flour
2 eggs
5 tablespoons sunflower oil
a little salt
1 cup milk
3 tablespoons butter, for frying*

*For the filling
2 pounds frozen spinach, thawed
8 ounces cream cheese
8 ounces Roquefort cheese
1 tablespoon chopped walnuts
1 teaspoon chervil*

*For the sauce
4 tablespoons butter
½ cup flour
1 pint milk
1 teaspoon whole-grain mustard
6 ounces Roquefort cheese
1 tablespoon finely chopped walnuts
1 tablespoon fresh chopped chervil, to
garnish*

Makes 16

1

Process the flour, eggs, oil and salt, slowly
adding milk until the mixture has the
consistency of light cream. (You may not
need to add all the milk.) Let the batter
rest in the refrigerator for 1 hour. Put
1 teaspoon of the butter in a frying pan
over the heat. Once it has melted, swirl it
around to coat the surface of the pan.

3

Cook the spinach over low heat for about
15 minutes. Drain off the water and let the
spinach cool. Process in a food processor
with the cream cheese and Roquefort until
smooth. Turn into a bowl and add the
walnuts and chervil for the filling.

2

Drop a heaping tablespoonful of batter into
the pan and tilt to spread it around evenly.
Cook until golden brown on the bottom,
then turn and cook briefly on the other
side. Lay the pancake on a wire rack. Cook
the others in the same way.

4

Preheat the oven to 375°F. Fill all the
pancakes and place in a shallow ovenproof
dish, rolled tightly and in rows. Make the
sauce by melting the butter, adding the
flour and cooking for a minute or two. Add
the milk and stir constantly until the sauce
comes to a boil. Stir in all the other
ingredients except the chervil. Pour the
sauce over the pancakes and bake for
20 minutes. Serve immediately, garnished
with chervil and the remaining walnuts.

Leek and Monkfish with Thyme Sauce

Monkfish is a well-known fish now, thanks to its excellent flavor and firm texture.

INGREDIENTS

2 pounds monkfish, cubed
salt and pepper
12 tablespoons butter
4 leeks, sliced
1 tablespoon flour
⅔ cup fish or
vegetable stock
2 teaspoons finely chopped fresh thyme,
plus more to garnish
juice of 1 lemon
⅔ cup light cream
radicchio, to garnish

Serves 4

1

Season the fish to taste. Melt about a third of the butter in a pan, and fry the fish for a short time. Set aside.

2

Fry the leeks in the pan with another third of the butter until they have softened. Set aside with the fish.

3

In a saucepan, melt the rest of the butter. Add the butter from the pan, stir in the flour, and add the stock. As the sauce thickens, add the thyme and lemon juice.

4

Return the leeks and monkfish to the pan and cook gently for a few minutes. Add the cream and season to taste. Serve immediately, garnished with thyme and radicchio leaves.

Fish Stew with Calvados, Parsley and Dill

This rustic stew harbors all sorts of interesting flavors and will please and intrigue. Many varieties of fish can be used, just choose the freshest and best.

INGREDIENTS

2 pounds assorted white fish
1 tablespoon chopped parsley, plus a
few leaves to garnish
8 ounces mushrooms
1 can (8 ounces) tomatoes
salt and pepper
2 teaspoons flour
1 tablespoon butter
2 cups cider
3 tablespoons Calvados
1 large bunch fresh dill sprigs,
reserving 4 fronds to garnish

Serves 4

1

Chop the fish roughly and place it in a casserole or stewing pot with the parsley, mushrooms and tomatoes, adding salt and pepper to taste.

2

Preheat the oven to 350°F. Work the flour into the butter. Heat the cider and stir in the flour and butter mixture a little at a time. Cook, stirring, until it has thickened slightly.

3

Add the cider mixture and the remaining ingredients to the fish and mix gently. Cover and bake for about 30 minutes. Serve garnished with sprigs of dill and parsley leaves.

Lamb and Leeks with Mint and Scallions

If you do not have any homemade chicken stock, use a good
quality ready-made stock rather than a bouillon cube.

INGREDIENTS

2 tablespoons sunflower oil
4 pounds lamb (fillet or boned leg),
cubed
10 scallions, thickly sliced
3 leeks, thickly sliced
1 tablespoon flour
²/₃ cup white wine
1¹/₃ cup chicken stock
1 tablespoon tomato paste
1 tablespoon sugar
salt and pepper
2 tablespoons fresh mint leaves, finely
chopped, plus a few more to garnish
4 ounces dried pears, chopped
2 pounds potatoes, peeled and sliced
2 tablespoons melted butter

Serves 6

1

Heat the oil and fry the cubed lamb
to seal it. Transfer to a casserole. Preheat
the oven to 350°F.

2

Fry the scallions and leeks for 1 minute,
stir in the flour and cook for another
minute. Add the wine and stock and bring
to a boil. Add the tomato paste, sugar, salt
and pepper with the mint and chopped
pears and pour into the casserole. Stir the
mixture. Arrange the sliced potatoes on top
and brush with the melted butter.

3

Cover and bake for 1½ hours. Then
increase the temperature to 400°F,
and cook for 30 more minutes,
uncovered, to brown the potatoes.
Garnish with mint leaves.

Stuffed Parsleyed Onions

Although devised as a vegetarian dish, these stuffed onions make a wonderful accompaniment to meat dishes, or an appetizing supper dish with crusty bread and a salad.

INGREDIENTS

4 large onions
4 tablespoons cooked rice
4 teaspoons finely chopped fresh
parsley, plus extra to garnish
4 tablespoons finely grated
sharp Cheddar cheese
salt and pepper
2 tablespoons olive oil
1 tablespoon white wine, to moisten

Serves 4

1

Cut a slice from the top of each onion and scoop out the center to leave a thick shell.

2

Combine all the remaining ingredients, moistening with enough wine to mix well. Preheat the oven to 350°F.

3

Fill the onions and bake for 45 minutes. Serve garnished with parsley.

Spring Roasted Chicken with Fresh Herbs and Garlic

A smaller chicken or four squabs can also be roasted in this way.

INGREDIENTS

4½ lb free-range chicken or
4 small squabs
finely grated rind and
juice of 1 lemon
1 garlic clove, crushed
2 tbsp olive oil
2 fresh thyme sprigs
2 fresh sage sprigs
6 tbsp unsalted butter,
softened
salt and freshly ground
black pepper

Serves 4

1

Season the chicken or squabs well.
Mix the lemon rind and juice, garlic and
olive oil together and pour them over the
chicken. Leave to marinate for at least
2 hours in a non-metallic dish.
When the chicken has marinated preheat
the oven to 450°F.

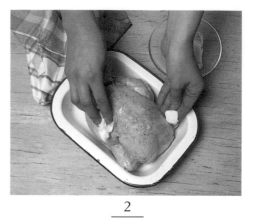

2

Place the herbs in the cavity of the bird and
smear the butter over the skin. Season well.
Roast the chicken for 10 minutes, then turn
the oven down to 375°F. Baste the chicken
well, and then roast for a further 1 hour
30 minutes, until the juices run clear when
the thigh is pierced with a skewer. Leave to
rest for 15 minutes before carving.

Lemon and Rosemary Lamb Chops

Spring lamb is delicious with the fresh flavor of lemon. Garnish with sprigs of
fresh rosemary — the aroma is irresistible.

INGREDIENTS

12 lamb chops
3 tbsp olive oil
2 large rosemary sprigs
juice of 1 lemon
3 garlic cloves, sliced
salt and freshly ground
black pepper

Serves 4

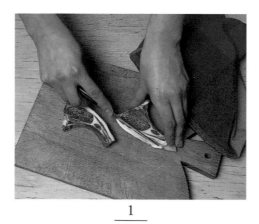

1

Trim the excess fat from the chops.
Mix the oil, rosemary, lemon juice and
garlic together and season well.
Preheat the broiler.

2

Pour over the chops in a shallow dish and
marinate for 30 minutes. Remove from the
marinade, and blot the excess with kitchen
paper and broil for 10 minutes on each side.

Carrot and Cilantro Soufflés

Use tender young carrots for this light-as-air dish.

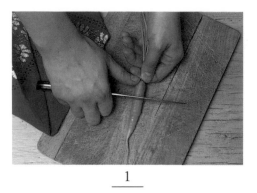

1

Peel the carrots.

2

Cook in boiling salted water for 20 minutes or until tender. Drain, and process until smooth in a food processor.

3

Preheat the oven to 400°F. Season the puréed carrots well, and stir in the chopped cilantro.

4

Fold the egg yolks into the carrot mixture.

5

In a separate bowl, whisk the egg whites until stiff.

6

Fold the egg whites into the carrot mixture and pour into four greased ramekins. Bake for about 20 minutes or until risen and golden. Serve immediately.

Leeks with Ham and Cheese Sauce

A tasty lunch or supper dish: use a strong cheese for best results.

INGREDIENTS

*4 leeks
4 slices ham*

*For the sauce
2 tbsp unsalted butter
1 tbsp all-purpose flour
1 ¼ cups milk
½ tsp French mustard
4 oz Cheddar cheese, grated
salt and freshly ground
black pepper*

Serves 4

1

Preheat the oven to 375°F. Trim the leeks to 1 in of the white and cook in salted water for about 20 minutes until soft. Drain thoroughly. Wrap the leeks in the ham slices.

2

To make the sauce, melt the butter in a saucepan. Add the flour and cook for a few minutes. Remove from the heat and gradually add the milk, whisking well with each addition. Return to the heat and whisk until the sauce thickens. Stir in the mustard and 3 oz of the cheese and season well. Lay the leeks in a shallow ovenproof dish and pour the sauce over. Scatter the extra cheese on top and bake for 20 minutes.

Baked Eggs with Heavy Cream and Chives

This is a rich dish best served with Melba toast: it's very easy and quick to make.

INGREDIENTS

*1 tbsp unsalted butter,
softened
4 tbsp heavy cream
1 tbsp chopped fresh chives
4 eggs
2 oz Gruyère cheese,
finely grated
salt and freshly ground
black pepper*

Serves 2

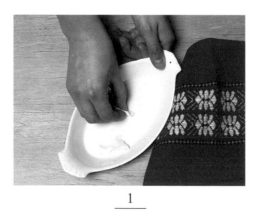

1

Preheat the oven to 350°F. Grease two individual gratin dishes. Mix the cream with the chives, and season with salt and pepper.

2

Break the eggs into each dish and top with the cream mixture. Sprinkle the cheese around the edges of the dishes and bake in the oven for 15–20 minutes. When cooked, brown the tops under the broiler for a minute.

Lemon Drizzle Cake

*You can also make this recipe using a large orange instead of the lemons;
either way, it makes a zesty treat for afternoon tea.*

INGREDIENTS

finely grated rind of 2 lemons
¾ cup superfine sugar
1 cup unsalted butter,
softened
4 eggs
2 cups self-rising flour
1 tsp baking powder
¼ tsp salt
shredded rind of 1 lemon,
and 1 tsp granulated sugar
to decorate

For the syrup
juice of 1 lemon
¾ cup superfine sugar

Serves 6

1

Preheat the oven to 325°F. Grease a 2 lb loaf
pan or 7–8 in round cake pan and line it with
wax paper or baking parchment. Mix the
lemon rind and superfine sugar together.

2

Cream the butter with the lemon and sugar
mixture. Add the eggs and mix until
smooth. Sift the flour, baking powder and
salt into a bowl and fold a third at a time into
the mixture. Turn the batter into the pan,
smooth the top and bake for 1½ hours or
until golden brown and springy to the touch.

3

To make the syrup, slowly heat the juice
with the sugar and dissolve it gently. Make
several slashes in the top of the cake and pour
the syrup over. Sprinkle the shredded lemon
rind and 1 tsp granulated sugar on top and
leave to cool.

Whole Wheat Bread

Homemade bread creates one of the most evocative smells in country cooking.
Eat this on the day you bake it, to enjoy the superb fresh taste.

INGREDIENTS

¾ oz fresh yeast
1¼ cups lukewarm milk
1 tsp superfine sugar
1½ cups whole wheat flour,
sifted
2 cups all-purpose white flour,
sifted
1 tsp salt
4 tbsp butter, chilled and cubed
1 egg, lightly beaten
2 tbsp mixed seeds

Makes 4 round loaves or
2 long loaves

1

Gently dissolve the yeast with a little of the milk and the sugar to make a paste. Place both the flours plus any bran from the sifter and the salt in a large warmed mixing bowl. Rub in the butter until the mixture resembles bread crumbs.

2

Add the yeast mixture, remaining milk and egg and mix into a fairly soft dough. Knead on a floured board for 15 minutes. Lightly grease the mixing bowl and put the dough back in the bowl, covering it with a piece of greased plastic wrap. Let rise until double in size in a warm place (this should take at least an hour).

3

Punch the dough down and knead it for a further 10 minutes. Preheat the oven to 400°F. To make round loaves, divide the dough into four pieces and shape them into flattish rounds. Place them on a floured baking sheet and let rise for a further 15 minutes. Sprinkle the loaves with the mixed seeds. Bake for about 20 minutes until golden and firm.

NOTE

For pan-shaped loaves, put the punched-down dough into two greased loaf pans instead. Let rise for a further 45 minutes and then bake for about 45 minutes, until the loaf sounds hollow when turned out of the pan and knocked on the base.

Rhubarb and Orange Crumble

*The almonds give this crumble topping a nutty taste and crunchy texture.
This crumble is extra-delicious with home-made custard.*

INGREDIENTS

2 lb rhubarb, cut in
2 in lengths
6 tbsp superfine sugar
finely grated rind and juice
of 2 oranges

1 cup all-purpose flour
½ cup unsalted butter,
chilled and cubed
6 tbsp demerara sugar
1¼ cups ground almonds

Serves 6

1

Preheat the oven to 350°F. Place the rhubarb
in a shallow ovenproof dish.

2

Sprinkle the superfine sugar over and add the
orange rind and juice.

3

Sift the flour into a mixing bowl and add the
butter. Rub the butter into the flour until
the mixture resembles bread crumbs.

4

Add the demerara sugar and ground almonds
and mix well.

5

Spoon the crumble mixture over the fruit to
cover it completely. Bake for 40 minutes,
until the top is browned and the fruit is
cooked. Serve warm.

Summer Recipes

....

*The warm, lazy days and light evenings of summer
provide the perfect excuse for outdoor dining
with friends and family. Try Mediterranean quiche
or a glorious green bean salad. Cooling treats
include strawberry fool, or homemade
mint ice cream.*

Herb and Chili Gazpacho

Gazpacho is a lovely soup, set off perfectly by the addition of a few herbs.

INGREDIENTS

2½ pounds ripe tomatoes
8 ounces onions
2 green peppers
1 green chili
1 large cucumber
2 tablespoons red wine vinegar
1 tablespoon balsamic vinegar
2 tablespoons olive oil
1 clove of garlic, peeled and crushed
⅓ cup tomato juice
2 tablespoons tomato paste
salt and pepper
2 tablespoons finely chopped mixed
fresh herbs, plus some extra to garnish

Serves 6

1

Set aside about a quarter of all the fresh vegetables, except the green chili, and place all the remaining ingredients in a food processor and season to taste. Process finely and chill in the refrigerator.

2

Chop the remaining vegetables and serve in a separate bowl to sprinkle over the soup. Crush some ice cubes and add to the center of each bowl. Garnish with fresh herbs. Serve with bread rolls.

Pear and Watercress Soup with Stilton Croutons

*Pears and Stilton taste very good when you eat them together after the main course—
here, for a change, they are served as an appetizer.*

INGREDIENTS

1 bunch watercress
4 medium pears, sliced
6 cups chicken stock, preferably
homemade
salt and pepper
½ cup heavy cream
juice of 1 lime

For the croutons
2 tablespoons butter
1 tablespoon olive oil
2 cups cubed stale bread
5 ounces chopped Stilton cheese

Serves 6

1

Set aside about a third of the
watercress leaves. Place all the rest of the
watercress leaves and stalks in a pan with
the pears, stock and a little seasoning.
Simmer for 15–20 minutes.

2

Reserving some watercress leaves for
garnishing, add the rest of the leaves and
immediately blend in a food processor until
smooth.

3

Put the mixture in a bowl and stir in the
cream and lime juice to mix the flavors
thoroughly. Season again to taste. Pour all
the soup back into a pan and reheat,
stirring gently until warmed through.

4

To make the croutons, melt the butter and
oil and fry the bread cubes until golden
brown. Drain on paper towels. Put the
cheese on top and heat under a hot broiler
until bubbling. Reheat the soup and pour
into bowls. Divide the croutons and
remaining watercress among the bowls.

Mackerel with Roasted Blueberries

Fresh blueberries burst with flavor when roasted, and their sharpness
complements the rich flesh of mackerel very well.

INGREDIENTS

2 tsp all-purpose flour
4 small cooked, smoked mackerel
4 tbsp unsalted butter
juice of ½ lemon
salt and freshly ground
black pepper

For the roasted blueberries
1 lb blueberries
2 tbsp superfine sugar
1 tbsp unsalted butter
salt and freshly ground
black pepper

Serves 4

1

Preheat the oven to 400°F. Season the flour. Dip each fish fillet into the flour to coat it well.

2

Dot the butter on the fillets and bake in the oven for 20 minutes.

3

Place the blueberries, sugar, butter and seasoning in a separate small roasting pan and roast them, basting them occasionally, for 15 minutes. To serve, drizzle the lemon juice over the roasted mackerel, accompanied by the roasted blueberries.

Pan-fried Trout with Bacon

This dish can also be cooked under the broiler.

INGREDIENTS

1 tbsp all-purpose flour
4 trout, cleaned and gutted
3 oz lean bacon
4 tbsp butter
1 tbsp olive oil
juice of ½ lemon
salt and freshly ground
black pepper

Serves 4

1

Pat the trout dry with paper towels and
mix the flour and seasoning together.

2

Roll the trout in the seasoned flour mixture
and wrap tightly in the bacon. Heat a
heavy frying pan. Heat the butter and
oil in the pan and fry the trout for 5 minutes
on each side. Serve immediately, with the
lemon juice drizzled on top.

Cod, Basil and Tomato with a Potato Thatch

With a green salad, this makes an ideal dish for lunch or a family supper.

INGREDIENTS

2 pounds smoked cod
2½ cups white cod
5 cups milk
2 sprigs basil
1 sprig lemon thyme
10 tablespoons butter
1 onion, peeled and chopped
¾ cup flour
2 tablespoons tomato paste
2 tablespoons chopped basil
12 medium-size old potatoes
1⅓ cups milk
salt and pepper
1 tablespoon chopped parsley

Serves 8

1

Place both kinds of fish in a roasting pan with the milk, 5 cups water and herbs. Simmer for 3–4 minutes. Let cool in the liquid for about 20 minutes. Drain the fish, reserving the liquid for use in the sauce. Flake the fish, taking care to remove any skin and bone, which should be discarded.

2

Melt 6 tablespoons butter in a pan, add the onion and cook for about 4 minutes, until tender but not browned. Add the flour, tomato paste and half the basil. Gradually add the reserved fish stock, adding a little more milk if necessary to make a fairly thin sauce. Bring this to a boil, season with salt and pepper, and add the remaining basil. Add the fish carefully and stir gently. Transfer to an ovenproof dish.

3

Preheat the oven to 350°F. Boil the potatoes until tender. Add the remaining 4 tablespoons butter and the milk, and mash well. Add salt and pepper to taste and cover the fish, using a fork to create a pattern. If you like, you can freeze the pie at this stage. Bake for 30 minutes. Serve with chopped parsley.

Lamb with Mint and Lemon

Lamb has been served with mint for many years – it is a great combination.

INGREDIENTS

8 lamb steaks, 8 ounces each
grated rind and juice of 1 lemon
2 cloves garlic, peeled and crushed
2 scallions, finely chopped
2 teaspoons finely chopped fresh mint
leaves, plus some leaves for
garnishing
4 tablespoons extra virgin olive oil
salt and black pepper

Serves 8

1

Make a marinade for the lamb by mixing all the other ingredients and seasoning to taste. Place the lamb steaks in a shallow dish and cover with the marinade. Refrigerate overnight.

2

Broil the lamb under high heat until just cooked, basting with the marinade occasionally during cooking. Turn once during cooking. Serve garnished with fresh mint leaves.

Mediterranean Quiche

The strong Mediterranean flavors of tomatoes, peppers and anchovies beautifully complement the cheese pastry in this unusual quiche.

INGREDIENTS

For the pastry
2 cups all-purpose flour
pinch of salt
pinch of mustard
½ cup butter, chilled and
cubed
2 oz Gruyère cheese, grated

For the filling
2 oz can of anchovies in oil,
drained
¼ cup milk
2 tbsp French mustard
3 tbsp olive oil
2 large Spanish onions, peeled
and sliced
1 red bell pepper, seeded and
very finely sliced
3 egg yolks
1 ½ cups heavy cream
1 garlic clove, crushed
6 oz sharp Cheddar
cheese, grated
2 large tomatoes, thickly sliced
salt and freshly ground
black pepper
2 tbsp chopped fresh basil,
to garnish

Serves 12

1

First make the pastry. Place the flour, salt and mustard in a food processor, add the butter and process the mixture until it resembles bread crumbs.

2

Add the cheese and process again briefly. Add enough iced water to make a stiff dough: it will be ready when the dough forms a ball. Wrap with plastic wrap and chill for 30 minutes.

3

Meanwhile, make the filling. Soak the anchovies in the milk for 20 minutes. Pour off the milk.

4

Roll out the chilled pastry and line a 9 in loose-based quiche pan. Spread the mustard over and chill for a further 15 minutes.

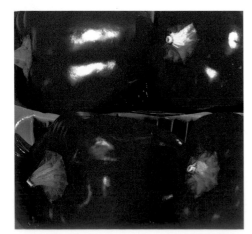

5

Preheat the oven to 400°F. Heat the oil in a frying pan and cook the onions and red pepper until soft. In a separate bowl, beat the egg yolks, cream, garlic and Cheddar cheese together; season well. Arrange the tomatoes in a single layer in the pastry crust. Top with the onion and pepper mixture and the anchovy fillets. Pour the egg mixture over. Bake for 30–35 minutes. Sprinkle over the basil and serve.

New Potato Salad

Potatoes freshly dug up from the garden are the best. Always leave the skins on: just wash the dirt away thoroughly. If you add the mayonnaise and other ingredients when the potatoes are hot, the flavors will develop as the potatoes cool.

INGREDIENTS

2 lb baby new potatoes
2 green apples, cored and chopped
4 scallions, chopped
3 celery stalks, finely chopped
2/3 cup homemade or storebought mayonnaise
salt and freshly ground black pepper

Serves 6

1

Cook the potatoes in salted, boiling water for about 20 minutes, or until they are very tender.

2

Drain the potatoes well and immediately add the remaining ingredients and stir until well mixed. Let cool and serve cold.

Green Bean Salad

The secret of this recipe is to dress the beans while still hot.

INGREDIENTS

6 oz cherry tomatoes, halved
1 tsp sugar
1 lb green beans, topped and tailed
6 oz feta cheese, cubed
salt and freshly ground black pepper

For the dressing
6 tbsp olive oil
3 tbsp white-wine vinegar
1/4 tsp Dijon mustard
2 garlic cloves, crushed
salt and freshly ground black pepper

Serves 6

1

Preheat the oven to 450°F. Put the cherry tomatoes on a baking sheet and sprinkle the sugar, salt and pepper over. Roast for 20 minutes, then let cool. Meanwhile, cook the beans in boiling salted water for 10 minutes.

2

Make the dressing by whisking together the oil, vinegar, mustard, garlic and seasoning. Drain the beans and immediately pour the vinaigrette over and mix well. When cool, stir in the roasted tomatoes and the feta cheese. Serve chilled.

Smoked Salmon and Dill Pasta

This has been tried and tested as both a main-dish salad and a starter, and the only preference stated was that as a main dish you got a larger portion.

INGREDIENTS

salt
12 ounces pasta twists
6 large sprigs fresh dill, chopped,
plus more sprigs to garnish
2 tablespoons extra virgin olive oil
1 tablespoon white wine vinegar
1⅓ cups heavy cream
pepper
6 ounces smoked salmon

Serves 2 as a main course

1

Boil the pasta in salted water until it is just cooked. Drain and run under the cold water until completely cooled. To make the dressing, combine all the remaining ingredients, apart from the smoked salmon and reserved dill, in the bowl of a food processor and blend well. Season to taste.

2

Slice the salmon into thin strips. Place the cooled pasta and the smoked salmon in a mixing bowl. Pour the dressing on top and toss carefully. Transfer to a serving bowl and garnish with the dill sprigs.

Avocado and Pasta Salad with Cilantro

Served as one of a variety of salads or alone, this tasty combination is sure to please.

INGREDIENTS

4 ounces pasta shells or bows
5 cups chicken stock
4 sticks celery, finely chopped
2 avocados, chopped
1 clove garlic, peeled and chopped
1 tablespoon finely chopped fresh cilantro,
plus some whole leaves to garnish
1 cup aged Cheddar cheese

For the dressing
⅔ cup extra virgin olive oil
1 tablespoon cider vinegar
2 tablespoons lemon juice
grated rind of 1 lemon
1 teaspoon French mustard
1 tablespoon chopped fresh cilantro
salt and pepper

Serves 4

1

Bring the chicken stock to a boil, add the pasta, and simmer for about 10 minutes, until just cooked. Drain and cool under cold running water.

2

Mix the celery, avocados, garlic and chopped cilantro in a bowl and add the cooled pasta. Sprinkle with the grated Cheddar.

3

Place all the ingredients for the dressing in a food processor and mix until the cilantro is finely chopped. Serve separately or pour over the salad and toss before serving. Garnish with cilantro leaves.

Country Strawberry Fool

*Make this delicious fool on the day you want to eat it, and chill it well,
for the best strawberry taste.*

INGREDIENTS

1 1/4 cups milk
2 egg yolks
scant 1/2 cup superfine
sugar
few drops of vanilla extract
2 lb ripe strawberries, stemmed
and washed
juice of 1/2 lemon
1 1/4 cups heavy cream

To decorate
12 small strawberries
4 fresh mint sprigs

Serves 4

1

First make the custard. Whisk 2 tbsp milk
with the egg yolks, 1 tbsp superfine sugar
and the vanilla extract.

2

Heat the remaining milk until it is just
below boiling point.

3

Stir the milk into the egg mixture. Rinse
the pan out and return the mixture to it.

4

Gently heat and stir until the custard
thickens enough to coat the back of a wooden
spoon. Lay a wet piece of wax paper on the
top of the custard and let it cool.

5

Purée the strawberries in a food processor or
blender with the lemon juice and the
remaining sugar.

6

Lightly whip the cream and fold in the fruit
purée and custard. Pour into glass dishes and
decorate with the whole strawberries and
sprigs of mint.

Mint Ice Cream

*This ice cream is best served slightly softened, so take it out
of the freezer 20 minutes before you want to serve it. For a special occasion,
this looks spectacular served in an ice bowl.*

INGREDIENTS

*8 egg yolks
6 tbsp superfine sugar
2½ cups light cream
1 vanilla bean
4 tbsp chopped fresh mint,
to garnish*

Serves 8

1

Beat the egg yolks and sugar until they are
pale and light using a hand-held electric
beater or a balloon whisk. Transfer to a
small saucepan.

2

In a separate saucepan, bring the cream to
a boil with the vanilla bean.

3

Remove the vanilla bean and pour the
hot cream on to the egg mixture,
whisking briskly.

4

Continue whisking to ensure the eggs
are mixed into the cream.

5

Gently heat the mixture until the custard
thickens enough to coat the back of a
wooden spoon. Let cool.

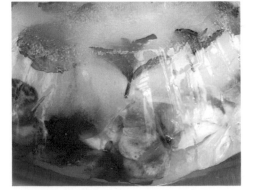

6

Stir in the mint and place in an ice-cream
maker to churn, about 3–4 hours. If you
don't have an ice-cream maker, freeze the
ice cream until mushy and then whisk it well
again, to break down the ice crystals. Freeze
for another 3 hours until it is softly frozen
and whisk again. Finally freeze until hard:
at least 6 hours.

Mixed Berry Tart

The orange-flavored pastry is delicious with the fresh fruits of summer.
Serve this with some extra shreds of orange rind scattered on top.

INGREDIENTS

For the pastry
2 cups all-purpose flour
½ cup unsalted butter
finely grated rind of 1 orange,
plus extra to decorate

For the filling
1¼ cups crème fraîche
and ¾ cup whipped cream
or ¾ cup sour cream
finely grated rind of 1 lemon
2 tsp confectioner's sugar
1½ lb mixed summer
berries

Serves 8

1

To make the pastry, put the flour and butter in a large bowl. Rub in the butter until the mixture resembles bread crumbs.

2

Add the orange rind and enough cold water to make a soft dough.

3

Roll into a ball and chill for at least 30 minutes. Roll out the pastry on a lightly floured surface.

4

Line a 9 in loose-based quiche pan with the pastry. Chill for 30 minutes. Preheat the oven to 400°F and place a baking sheet in the oven to heat up. Line the pan with wax paper and baking beans and bake blind on the baking sheet for 15 minutes. Remove the paper and beans and bake for 10 minutes more, until the pastry is golden. Allow to cool completely. To make the filling, whisk the crème fraîche, lemon rind and sugar together and pour into the pastry crust. Top with fruit, sprinkle with orange rind and serve sliced.

Autumn Recipes

Reap the benefits of the autumn harvest with this collection of recipes; wild mushroom tart, thyme-roasted onions and chicken with sloe gin and juniper all make the most of autumn produce. Warming desserts such as blackberry charlotte and apple tart are guaranteed to keep away the autumn chill.

Wild Mushroom Tart

The flavor of wild mushrooms makes this tart really rich: use as wide a variety of mushrooms as you can get.

INGREDIENTS

For the pastry
2 cups all-purpose flour
4 tbsp Crisco
2 tsp lemon juice
about ⅔ cup ice water
½ cup butter, chilled and
cubed
1 egg, beaten, to glaze

For the filling
10 tbsp butter
2 shallots, finely chopped
2 garlic cloves, crushed
1 lb mixed wild mushrooms such as
porcini, oyster mushrooms, or
shiitake mushrooms, sliced
3 tbsp chopped fresh parsley
2 tbsp heavy cream
salt and freshly ground
black pepper

Serves 6

1

To make the pastry, sift the flour and
½ tsp salt together into a large bowl.
Add the Crisco and rub into the mixture
until it resembles bread crumbs.

2

Add the lemon juice and enough ice water
to make a soft but not sticky dough.
Cover and chill for 20 minutes.

3

Roll the pastry out into a rectangle on a
lightly floured surface. Mark the dough into
three equal strips and arrange half the butter
cubes over two-thirds of the dough.

5

Chill the pastry for 20 minutes. Repeat the
process of marking into thirds, folding over,
giving a quarter turn and rolling out three
times, chilling for 20 minutes in between
each time. To make the filling, melt
4 tbsp butter and fry the shallots and garlic
until soft but not browned. Add the
remaining butter and the mushrooms and
cook for 35–40 minutes. Drain off any excess
liquid and stir in the remaining ingredients.
Let cool. Preheat the oven to 450°F.

4

Fold the outer two-thirds over, folding over
the uncovered third last. Seal the edges with
a rolling pin. Give the dough a quarter turn
and roll it out again. Mark it into thirds and
dot with the remaining butter cubes
in the same way.

6

Divide the pastry in two. Roll out one half
into a 9 in round, cutting around a plate to
make a neat shape. Pile the filling into the
center. Roll out the remaining pastry large
enough to cover the base. Brush the edges of
the base with water and then lay the second
pastry circle on top. Press the edges together
to seal and brush the top with a little beaten
egg. Bake for 45 minutes, or until the pastry
is risen, golden and flaky.

Mushroom and Parsley Soup

*Thickened with bread, this rich mushroom soup will warm you up
on cold autumn days. It makes a terrific hearty lunch.*

INGREDIENTS

6 tbsp unsalted butter
2 lb mushrooms, trimmed, wiped
and sliced
2 onions, coarsely chopped
2½ cups milk
8 slices white bread
4 tbsp chopped fresh parsley
1¼ cups heavy cream
salt and freshly ground
black pepper

Serves 8

1

Melt the butter and sauté the mushrooms
and onions until soft but not colored –
about 10 minutes. Add the milk.

2

Tear the bread into pieces, drop them into
the soup and let the bread soak for
15 minutes. Purée the soup and return it to
the pan. Add the parsley, cream and seasoning.
Reheat, but do not allow the soup to boil.
Serve at once.

Thyme-roasted Onions

*These slowly roasted onions develop a delicious sweet flavor which is delicious
with roast meat. You could prepare parboiled new potatoes in the same way.*

INGREDIENTS

5 tbsp olive oil
4 tbsp unsalted butter
2 lb small onions
2 tbsp chopped fresh thyme
salt and freshly ground
black pepper

Serves 4

1

Preheat the oven to 425°F. Heat the oil
and butter in a large roasting pan. Add
the onions and toss them in the oil and
butter mixture.

2

Add the thyme and seasoning and roast for
45 minutes, basting regularly.

Spinach, Cognac, Garlic and Chicken Pâté

INGREDIENTS

12 slices bacon
2 tablespoons butter
1 onion, peeled and chopped
1 clove garlic, peeled and crushed
10 ounces frozen spinach, thawed
½ cup whole-wheat bread crumbs
2 tablespoons Cognac
1 pound ground chicken
(dark and light meat)
1 pound ground pork
2 eggs, beaten
2 tablespoons chopped mixed fresh
herbs, such as parsley, sage and dill
salt and pepper

Serves 12

1

Fry the bacon in a pan until it is only just done, then arrange it around the sides of a 3½-cup loaf pan, leaving a couple of slices to garnish if posssible.

3

Preheat the oven to 350°F. Combine all the remaining ingredients, apart from any remaining bacon strips, in a bowl and mix well to blend. Spoon the pâté into the loaf pan and cover with any remaining bacon.

2

Melt the butter. Fry the onion and garlic until soft. Squeeze the spinach to remove as much water as possible, then add to the pan, stirring until the spinach is dry.

4

Cover the pan with a double thickness of foil and set it in a baking pan. Pour 1 inch boiling water into the baking pan. Bake for about 1¼ hours. Remove the pâté and let it cool. Place a heavy weight on top of the pâté and refrigerate overnight.

Beef, Celeriac and Horseradish Pâté

INGREDIENTS

1 pound topside of beef, cubed
1½ cups red wine
⅜ cup Madeira
1 cup beef or chicken stock
2 tablespoons finely chopped celeriac
1 tablespoon horseradish cream
salt and pepper
2 bay leaves
2 tablespoons brandy
12 tablespoons butter, melted

Serves 4

1

Preheat the oven to 250°F. Place the beef in a casserole. Combine all the other ingredients except the brandy and butter, and pour them over the beef. Cover tightly and cook for 2 hours.

3

Melt the remaining butter, skim any foam off the top and pour over the top of the beef, leaving any residue at the bottom of the pan. Cover the pâté and refrigerate overnight.

2

Remove and drain. Strain the liquid and reduce to about 3 tablespoons. Slice and roughly chop the meat and put it with the reduced liquid in the food processor. Blend until fairly smooth. Add the brandy and a third of the butter. Turn into a pâté dish and let cool.

Chicken Stew with Blackberries and Lemon Balm

INGREDIENTS

4 chicken breasts, partly boned
salt and pepper
scant 2 tablespoons butter
1 tablespoon sunflower oil
4 tablespoons flour
⅔ cup red wine
⅔ cup chicken stock
grated rind of half an orange plus
1 tablespoon juice
3 sprigs lemon balm, finely chopped,
plus 1 sprig to garnish
⅔ cup heavy cream
1 egg yolk
4 ounces fresh blackberries,
2 ounces to garnish

Serves 4

1

Remove any skin from the chicken, and season the meat. Heat the butter and oil in a pan, fry the chicken to seal it, then transfer to a casserole dish. Stir the flour into the pan, then add wine and stock and bring to a boil. Add the orange rind and juice, and also the chopped lemon balm. Pour over the chicken.

2

Preheat the oven to 350°F. Cover the casserole and bake for about 40 minutes.

3

Blend the cream with the egg yolk, add some of the liquid from the casserole and stir the mixture back into the dish with the blackberries (reserving the ones for the garnish). Cover and cook for another 10–15 minutes. Serve garnished with the rest of the blackberries and lemon balm.

Pork and Mushrooms with Sage and Mango Chutney

INGREDIENTS

scant 2 tablespoons butter
1 tablespoon sunflower oil
1½ pounds cubed pork
6 ounces onion, peeled and
chopped
2 tablespoons flour
2 cups stock
4 tablespoons white wine
salt and pepper
8 ounces mushrooms, sliced
6 fresh sage leaves, finely chopped
2 tablespoons mango chutney
1 fresh mango, peeled and sliced, to
garnish

Serves 4

1

Heat the butter and oil and fry the pork in a pan to seal it. Transfer to a casserole. Fry the onion in the pan, stir in the flour and cook for 1 minute. Preheat the oven to 350°F.

2

Gradually add the stock and white wine to the onion and bring to a boil. Season well and add the mushrooms, sage leaves and mango chutney. Pour the sauce mixture over the pork and cover the casserole. Bake for about 1 hour, depending on the cut of pork, until tender. Check the seasoning, garnish with mango slices, and serve with rice.

Chicken with Sloe Gin and Juniper

Juniper is used in the manufacture of gin, and this dish is flavored with both sloe gin and juniper. Sloe gin is easy to make and has a wonderful flavor, but it can also be bought ready-made.

INGREDIENTS

2 tablespoons butter
2 tablespoons sunflower oil
8 chicken breast fillets
12 ounces carrots, cooked
1 clove garlic, peeled and crushed
1 tablespoon finely chopped parsley
¼ cup chicken stock
¼ cup red wine
¼ cup sloe gin
1 teaspoon crushed juniper berries
salt and pepper
1 bunch basil, to garnish

Serves 8

1

Melt the butter with the oil in a pan, and sauté the chicken fillets until they are browned on all sides.

2

In a food processor, combine all the remaining ingredients except the basil, and blend to a smooth puree. If the mixture seems too thick, add a little more red wine or water until a thinner consistency is reached.

3

Put the chicken breasts in a pan, pour the sauce over the top and cook until the chicken is cooked through, which should take about 15 minutes. Adjust the seasoning and serve garnished with chopped fresh basil leaves.

Spicy Duck Breasts with Red Plums

Duck breasts can be bought separately, which makes this dish very easy to prepare.

INGREDIENTS

*4 duck breasts, 6 ounces
each, skinned
salt
2 teaspoons crushed stick cinnamon
4 tablespoons butter
1 tablespoon plum brandy (or Cognac)
1 cup chicken stock
1 cup heavy cream
pepper
6 fresh red plums, pitted and sliced
6 sprigs cilantro leaves, plus some
extra to garnish*

Serves 4

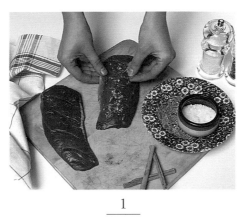

1

Preheat the oven to 375°F. Score the duck breasts and sprinkle with salt. Press the crushed cinnamon onto both sides of the duck breasts. Melt half the butter in a pan and fry them on both sides to seal, then place in an ovenproof dish with the butter and bake for 6–7 minutes.

2

Remove the dish from the oven and return the contents to the pan. Add the brandy and set it alight. When the flames have died down, remove from the pan and keep warm. Add the stock and cream to the pan and simmer gently until reduced and thick. Adjust the seasoning.

3

Reserve a few plum slices for garnishing. In a pan, melt the other half of the butter and fry the plums and cilantro, just enough to cook the fruit through. Slice the duck breasts and pour some sauce around each one, then garnish with slices of plum and chopped cilantro.

Stuffed Tomatoes with Wild Rice, Corn and Cilantro

These tomatoes could be served as a light meal or as an accompaniment for meat or fish.

INGREDIENTS

8 medium tomatoes
¼ cup corn kernels
2 tablespoons white wine
¼ cup cooked wild rice
1 clove garlic
¼ cup grated Cheddar cheese
1 tablespoon chopped fresh cilantro
salt and pepper
1 tablespoon olive oil

Serves 4

1

Cut the tops off the tomatoes and remove the seeds with a small spoon. Scoop out all the flesh and chop finely—remember to chop the tops as well.

2

Preheat the oven to 350°F. Put the chopped tomato in a pan. Add the corn and the white wine. Cover with a close-fitting lid and simmer until tender. Drain the excess liquid.

3

Combine all the remaining ingredients except the olive oil, adding salt and pepper to taste. Carefully spoon the mixture into the tomatoes, piling it higher in the center. Sprinkle the oil over the top, arrange the tomatoes in an ovenproof dish and bake at 350°F for 15–20 minutes, until cooked through.

Spinach, Walnut and Gruyère Lasagne with Basil

This nutty lasagne is a delicious combination of flavors that easily equals the traditional meat and tomato version.

INGREDIENTS

*12 ounces spinach lasagne
(quick cooking)*

For the walnut and tomato sauce
*3 tablespoons walnut oil
1 large onion, chopped
8 ounces celeriac, finely chopped
1 can (14 ounces) chopped tomatoes
1 large clove garlic, finely chopped
½ teaspoon sugar
1 cup chopped walnuts
⅔ cup Dubonnet
salt and pepper*

For the spinach and Gruyère sauce
*6 tablespoons butter
2 tablespoons walnut oil
1 medium onion, chopped
¾ cup flour
1 teaspoon mustard powder
5 cups milk
2 cups grated Gruyère cheese
salt and pepper
ground nutmeg
1 pound frozen spinach,
thawed and puréed
2 tablespoons basil, chopped*

Serves 8

1

First make the walnut and tomato sauce. Heat the walnut oil and sauté the onion and celeriac. Cook for 8–10 minutes. Meanwhile, puree the tomatoes in a food processor. Add the garlic to the pan and cook for about 1 minute, then add the sugar, walnuts, tomatoes and Dubonnet. Season to taste. Simmer, uncovered, for 25 minutes.

2

To make the spinach and Gruyère sauce, melt the butter with the walnut oil and add the onion. Cook for 5 minutes, then stir in the flour. Cook for another minute and add the mustard powder and milk, stirring vigorously. When the sauce has come to a boil, take off the heat and add three-quarters of the grated Gruyère. Season to taste with salt, pepper and nutmeg. Finally, add the puréed spinach.

3

Preheat the oven to 350°F. Layer the lasagne in an ovenproof dish. Start with a layer of the spinach and Gruyère sauce, then add a little walnut and tomato sauce, then a layer of lasagne, and continue until the dish is full, ending with a layer of either sauce. Sprinkle the remaining Gruyère over the top of the dish, followed by the basil. Bake for 45 minutes.

Cheese Scones

These delicious scones make a good tea-time or brunch treat. They are best served fresh and still slightly warm.

INGREDIENTS

2 cups all-purpose flour
2¹/₂ tsp baking powder
¹/₂ tsp mustard powder
¹/₂ tsp salt
4 tbsp butter, chilled and cubed
3 oz Cheddar cheese, grated
²/₃ cup milk
1 egg, beaten

Makes 12

1

Preheat the oven to 450°F. Sift the flour, baking powder, mustard powder and salt into a mixing bowl. Add the butter and rub it into the flour mixture until the mixture resembles bread crumbs. Stir in 2 oz of the cheese.

2

Make a well in the center and add the milk and egg. Mix gently and then turn the dough out on to a lightly floured surface. Roll it out and cut it into triangles or squares. Brush lightly with milk and sprinkle with the remaining cheese. Let rest for 15 minutes, then bake them for 15 minutes, or until well risen.

Oatcakes

These are very simple to make and are an excellent addition to a cheese board.

INGREDIENTS

1²/₃ cups oatmeal
³/₄ cup all-purpose flour
¹/₄ tsp baking soda
tsp salt
2 tbsp Crisco
2 tbsp butter

Makes 24

1

Preheat the oven to 425°F. Place the oatmeal, flour, soda and salt in a large bowl. Gently melt the Crisco and butter together in a pan.

2

Add the melted fat and enough boiling water to make a soft dough. Turn out on to a surface scattered with a little oatmeal. Roll out the dough thinly and cut it into circles. Bake the oatcakes on ungreased baking sheets for 15 minutes, until crisp.

Blackberry Charlotte

A classic dessert, perfect for cold days. Serve with lightly whipped cream or homemade custard.

INGREDIENTS

5 tbsp unsalted butter
3 cups fresh white bread crumbs
4 tbsp brown sugar
4 tbsp maple syrup
finely grated rind and juice
of 2 lemons
2 oz walnut halves
1 lb blackberries
1 lb cooking apples, peeled,
cored and finely sliced
whipped cream or
custard, to serve

Serves 4

1

Preheat the oven to 350°F. Grease a 2 cup
Pyrex dish with 1 tbsp of the butter. Melt the
remaining butter and add the bread crumbs.
Sauté them for 5–7 minutes, until the
crumbs are slightly crisp and golden.
Leave to cool slightly.

2

Place the sugar, syrup, lemon rind and juice
in a small saucepan and gently warm them.
Add the crumbs.

3

Process the walnuts until they are
finely ground.

4

Arrange a thin layer of blackberries in the
dish. Top with a thin layer of crumbs.

5

Add a thin layer of apple, topping it with
another thin layer of crumbs. Repeat the
process with another layer of blackberries,
followed by a layer of crumbs. Continue
until you have used up all the ingredients,
finishing with a layer of crumbs.
The mixture should be piled well above
the top edge of the dish, because it shrinks
during cooking. Bake for 30 minutes, until
the crumbs are golden and the fruit is soft.

French Apple Tart

For added flavor, scatter some slivered almonds over the top of this classic tart.

INGREDIENTS

For the pastry
½ cup unsalted butter,
softened
4 tbsp vanilla sugar
1 egg
2 cups all-purpose flour

For the filling
4 tbsp unsalted butter
5 large tart apples, peeled, cored
and sliced
juice of ½ lemon
1¼ cups heavy cream
2 egg yolks
2 tbsp vanilla sugar
⅔ cup ground almonds,
toasted
2 tbsp slivered almonds, toasted,
to garnish

Serves 8

1

Place the butter and sugar in a food processor and process them well together. Add the egg and process to mix it in well.

2

Add the flour and process till you have a soft dough. Wrap the dough in plastic wrap and chill it for 30 minutes.

3

Roll the pastry out on a lightly floured surface to about 9–10 in diameter.

4

Line a pie pan with the pastry and chill it for a further 30 minutes. Preheat the oven to 425°F and place a baking sheet in the oven to heat up. Line the pastry case with wax paper and baking beans and bake blind on the baking sheet for 10 minutes. Then remove the beans and paper and cook for a further 5 minutes.

5

Turn the oven down to 375°F. To make the filling, melt the butter in a frying pan and lightly sauté the apples for 5–7 minutes. Sprinkle the apples with lemon juice.

6

Beat the cream and egg yolks with the sugar. Stir in the toasted ground almonds. Arrange the apple slices on top of the warm pastry and pour over the cream mixture. Bake for 25 minutes, or until the cream is just about set – it tastes better if the cream is still slightly runny in the center. Serve hot or cold, scattered with slivered almonds.

Winter Recipes

....

*With the nights drawing in, we all need something
substantial and warming to keep out the cold. Try
roast beef with roasted peppers, or raised country pie.
Country pancakes or cranberry muffins are a
perfect fire-side treat, and rich Christmas pudding
is the perfect way to round off the year.*

Roast Beef with Porcini and Sweet Bell Peppers

A substantial and warming dish for cold, dark evenings.

INGREDIENTS

3–3½ lb piece of sirloin
1 tbsp olive oil
1 lb small red bell peppers
4 oz mushrooms
6 oz thick-sliced pancetta
or bacon, cubed
2 tbsp all-purpose flour
⅔ cup full-bodied
red wine
1¼ cups beef stock
2 tbsp Marsala
2 tsp dried mixed herbs
salt and freshly ground
black pepper

Serves 8

1

Preheat the oven to 375°F. Season the meat well. Heat the olive oil in a large frying pan. When very hot, brown the meat on all sides. Place in a large roasting pan and cook for 1¼ hours.

2

Put the red peppers in the oven to roast for 20 minutes, if small ones are available, or 45 minutes if large ones are used.

3

Near the end of the meat's cooking time, prepare the gravy. Coarsely chop the mushroom caps and stems.

4

Heat the frying pan again and add the pancetta or bacon. Cook until the fat runs freely from the meat. Add the flour and cook for a few minutes until browned.

5

Gradually stir in the red wine and the stock. Bring to a boil, stirring. Lower the heat and add the Marsala, herbs and seasoning.

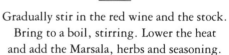

6

Add the mushrooms to the pan and heat through. Remove the sirloin from the oven and leave to stand for 10 minutes before carving it. Serve with the roasted peppers and the hot gravy.

Bacon and Lentil Soup

Serve this hearty soup with chunks of warm, crusty bread.

INGREDIENTS

*1 lb thick-sliced bacon,
cubed
1 onion, coarsely chopped
1 small turnip, coarsely chopped
1 celery stalk, chopped
1 carrot, sliced
1 potato, peeled and
coarsely chopped
1/2 cup lentils
1 bouquet garni
freshly ground black pepper*

Serves 4

1

Heat a large pan and add the bacon. Cook for
a few minutes, allowing the fat to run out.

2

Add all the vegetables and cook for
4 minutes.

3

Add the lentils, bouquet garni, seasoning
and enough water to cover. Bring to a boil
and simmer for 1 hour, or until the lentils
are tender.

Creamy Layered Potatoes

Cook the potatoes on top of the stove first to help the dish to bake more quickly.

3–3½ lb large potatoes, peeled
and sliced
2 large onions, sliced
6 tbsp unsalted butter
1¼ cups heavy cream
salt and freshly ground
black pepper

Serves 6

1

Preheat the oven to 400°F. Blanch the sliced
potatoes for 2 minutes, and drain well.

2

Place the potatoes, onions, butter and cream
in a pan, stir well and cook for about
15 minutes. Transfer to a large ovenproof
dish, season well and bake for 1 hour, until
the potatoes are tender.

Traditional Beef Stew and Dumplings

This dish can cook in the oven while you go for a wintery walk to work up an appetite.

INGREDIENTS

1 tbsp all-purpose flour
2½ lb stewing beef,
cubed
2 tbsp olive oil
2 large onions, sliced
1 lb carrots, sliced
½ pint / 1¼ cups Guinness
or dark beer
3 bay leaves
2 tsp brown sugar
3 fresh thyme sprigs
1 tsp cider vinegar
salt and freshly ground
black pepper

For the dumplings
½ cup chopped Crisco
2 cups self-rising
flour
2 tbsp chopped mixed
fresh herbs
about ⅔ cup water

Serves 6

1

Preheat the oven to 325°F. Season the flour and sprinkle over the meat, tossing to coat.

2

Heat the oil in a large casserole and lightly sauté the onions and carrots. Remove the vegetables with a slotted spoon and reserve them.

3

Brown the meat well in batches in the casserole.

4

Return all the vegetables to the casserole and add any leftover seasoned flour. Add the Guinness or beer, bay leaves, sugar and thyme. Bring the liquid to a boil and then transfer to the oven.

5

After the meat has been cooking for 1 hour and 40 minutes, make the dumplings. Mix the Crisco and flour together. Add enough water to make a soft, sticky dough.

6

Form the dough into small balls with floured hands. Add the cider vinegar to the meat and spoon the dumplings on top. Cook for a further 20 minutes, until the dumplings have cooked through and serve hot.

Country Pie

A classic raised pie. It takes quite a long time to make,
but is a perfect winter treat.

INGREDIENTS

1 small duck
1 small chicken
12 oz pork belly, minced
1 egg, lightly beaten
2 shallots, finely chopped
½ tsp ground cinnamon
½ tsp grated nutmeg
1 tsp Worcestershire sauce
finely grated rind of 1 lemon
½ tsp freshly ground black pepper
⅔ cup red wine
6 oz ham, cut into cubes
salt and freshly ground
black pepper

For the aspic
all the meat bones and trimmings
2 carrots
1 onion
2 celery stalks
1 tbsp red wine
1 bay leaf
1 whole clove
1 packet of gelatin
(about 1 oz)

For the pastry
1 cup Crisco
1¼ cups boiling water
6 cups all-purpose flour
1 egg, lightly beaten with a
pinch of salt

Serves 12

1

Cut as much meat from the raw duck and chicken as possible, removing the skin and sinews. Cut the duck and chicken breasts into cubes and set them aside.

2

Mix the rest of the duck and chicken meat with the minced pork, egg, shallots, spices, Worcestershire sauce, lemon rind and salt and pepper. Add the red wine and leave for about 15 minutes for the flavors to develop.

3

To make the aspic, place the meat bones and trimmings, carrots, onion, celery, wine, bay leaf and clove in a large pan and cover with 12½ cups of water. Bring to a boil, skimming off any scum, and simmer gently for 2½ hours.

4

To make the pastry, place the fat and water in a pan and bring to a boil. Sift the flour with a pinch of salt into a bowl and pour on the hot liquid. Mix with a wooden spoon, and, when the dough is cool enough to handle, knead it well and let it sit in a warm place, covered with a cloth, for 20–30 minutes or until you are ready to use it. Preheat the oven to 400°F.

5

Grease a 10 in loose-based deep cake pan. Roll out about two-thirds of the pastry thinly enough to line the cake pan. Make sure there are no holes and allow enough pastry to leave a little hanging over the top. Fill the pie with a layer of half the minced-pork mixture; then top this with a layer of the cubed duck and chicken breast-meat and cubes of ham. Top with the remaining minced pork. Brush the overhanging edges of pastry with water and cover with the remaining rolled-out pastry. Seal the edges well. Make two large holes in the top and decorate with any pastry trimmings.

6

Bake the pie for 30 minutes. Brush the top with the egg and salt mixture. Turn down the oven to 350°F. After 30 minutes loosely cover the pie with foil to prevent the top getting too brown, and bake it for a further 1 hour.

7

Strain the stock after 2½ hours. Let it cool and remove the solidified layer of fat from the surface. Measure 2½ cups of stock. Heat it gently to just below boiling point and whisk the gelatin into it until no lumps are left. Add the remaining strained stock and leave to cool.

8

When the pie is cool, place a funnel through one of the holes and pour in as much of the stock as possible, letting it come up to the holes in the crust. Leave to set for at least 24 hours before slicing and serving.

Leek and Onion Tart

This unusual recipe isn't a normal tart with pastry, but an all-in-one savory slice that is excellent served as an accompaniment to roast meat.

INGREDIENTS

4 tbsp unsalted butter
12 oz leeks, sliced thinly
2 cups self-rising flour
½ cup Crisco
⅔ cup water
salt and freshly ground
black pepper

Serves 4

1

Preheat the oven to 400°F. Melt the butter in a pan and sauté the leeks until soft. Season well.

2

Mix the flour, fat and water together in a bowl to make a soft but sticky dough. Mix into the leek mixture in the pan. Place in a greased shallow ovenproof dish and bake for 30 minutes, or until brown and crispy. Serve sliced, as a vegetable accompaniment.

Orange Shortbread Fingers

These are a real tea-time treat. The fingers will keep in an airtight tin for up to two weeks.

INGREDIENTS

½ cup unsalted butter,
softened
4 tbsp superfine sugar,
plus a little extra
finely grated rind of 2 oranges
1½ cups all-purpose flour

Makes 18

1

Preheat the oven to 375°F. Beat the butter and sugar together until they are soft and creamy. Beat in the orange rind.

2

Gradually add the flour and gently pull the dough together to form a soft ball. Roll the dough out on a lightly floured surface until about ½ in thick. Cut it into fingers, sprinkle over a little extra superfine sugar, prick with a fork and bake for about 20 minutes, or until the fingers are a light golden color.

Cranberry Muffins

A tea or breakfast dish that is not too sweet.

INGREDIENTS

3 cups all-purpose flour
1 tsp baking powder
pinch of salt
¹/₂ cup superfine sugar
2 eggs
²/₃ cup milk
4 tbsp corn oil
finely grated rind of 1 orange
5 oz cranberries

Makes 12

1

Preheat the oven to 375°F. Line a muffin
pan with paper cases. Mix the flour, baking
powder, salt and superfine sugar together.

2

Lightly beat the eggs with the milk and oil.
Add them to the dry ingredients and blend
to make a smooth batter. Stir in the orange
rind and cranberries. Divide the mixture
between the muffin cases and bake for
25 minutes until risen and golden.
Let cool in the pan for a few minutes, and
serve warm or cold.

Country Pancakes

Serve these hot with butter and maple syrup or jam.

INGREDIENTS

2 cups self-rising flour
4 tbsp superfine sugar
4 tbsp butter, melted
1 egg
1 ¹/₄ cups milk
1 tbsp corn oil or
margarine

Makes 24

1

Mix the flour and sugar together. Add the
melted butter and egg with two-thirds of the
milk. Mix to a smooth batter – it should be
thin enough to find its own level.

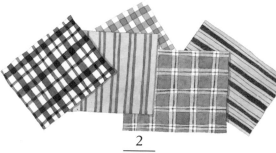

2

Heat a griddle or a heavy-based frying pan
and wipe it with a little oil or margarine.
When hot, drop spoonfuls of the mixture
on to the hot griddle or pan. When bubbles
come to the surface of the pancakes, flip them
over to cook until golden on the other side.
Keep the pancakes warm wrapped in a dish
towel while cooking the rest of the mixture.
Serve as soon as possible.

Christmas Pudding

The classic Christmas dessert. Wrap it in cheesecloth and store it in an airtight container for up to a year for the flavors to develop.

INGREDIENTS

1 cup all-purpose flour
pinch of salt
1 tsp ground allspice
½ tsp ground cinnamon
¼ tsp freshly grated nutmeg
1 cup grated hard Crisco
1 apple, grated
2 cups fresh white
bread crumbs
1⅞ cups soft brown
sugar
2 oz slivered almonds
1½ cups seedless raisins
1½ cups currants
1½ cups golden raisins
4 oz ready-to-eat dried
apricots
¾ cup chopped mixed
citrus peel
finely grated rind and juice
of 1 lemon
2 tbsp molasses
3 eggs
1¼ cups milk
2 tbsp rum

Serves 8

1
Sift the flour, salt and spices into
a large bowl.

2
Add the Crisco, apple and other dry
ingredients, including the grated
lemon rind.

3
Heat the molasses until warm and runny
and pour into the dry ingredients.

4
Mix together the eggs, milk, rum
and lemon juice.

5
Stir the liquid into the dry mixture.

6
Spoon the mixture into two 5 cup bowls.
Wrap the puddings with pieces of wax paper,
pleated to allow for expansion, and tie with
string. Steam the puddings in a steamer or
saucepan of boiling water. Each pudding
needs 10 hours' cooking and 3 hours'
reheating. Remember to keep the water level
topped up to keep the pans from boiling dry.
Serve decorated with holly.

Index